ON REFLECTION

A Look At Life In Prose And Poetry

By

Pat Abercromby
and Friends

Hope this brings you pleasure Love Moyra x

Dedicated to the memory of Diane McAdam
11 March 1942 to 11 October 2019

'She knew how to do friendship'
– Frances Burns, OBE

All good wishes Sarah

CONTENTS

ACKNOWLEDGMENTS

This anthology was breathed into life by the efforts of an enthusiastic group of women writers I am privileged to call my friends.

Many thanks to Jane MacKinnon and Sarah-Jane Reeve not only for their contributions of prose and poetry but also for their invaluable editing skills.

Thanks also to Moyra Zaman, Louise Norton, Barbara Kuessner Hughes, Kim Abercromby, Anne Silk, Charlene K. Haar, Elizabeth A. Prais and Libby Evans for their contributions of short stories and poetry.

Special thanks too, to Libby Evans who also created the illustrations.

FOREWORD

We invite you, the reader, to dip into this anthology
of short stories and poetry. Between these pages, you
will find shared glimpses of life and love, reflected
through the imaginations and eyes of women writers,
all linked by friendship and a love of the written
word.

1. Off-Centre

SHAITANA

Barbara Kuessner Hughes

There's nothing to do but wait. Shaitana stretches her lithe form as far as the airless space will allow and flexes a slender wrist. She wasn't trapped here by chance, didn't simply grow like a seed in the chink of a wall. How long has it been since she last had a chance to fulfil her function?

***

On a sparkling Saturday morning, Mandy is relishing the novelty of city life. In her mind, weekends in the country never held as much promise. A day of leisure stretches ahead of her and Russell but, as is frequently the case on Mandy's treasured weekends, he's being grumpy; a combination of work stress and last night's hangover. This morning he looks like a bear with a beard, and not much more approachable.

'Why don't we go to the café on the corner and have breakfast?' Mandy suggests. 'Maybe some food and strong coffee will make you feel better.'

Russell gives a reply which is not much more than a grunt but follows her as she leads the way. They occupy an alcove by a window and observe as a good random sampling of the human race passes along the street outside. Mandy tries not to count how many couples are strolling about in little personal oases of romance, arms draped around one another. Her gaze falls on Russell's large fingers, which are stretched out on the tabletop. *How long has it been since we've held hands?* Mandy wonders suddenly. She reaches out towards Russell, but yawning cavernously, staring out of the window, he pulls his arms away, and they slip beneath the table.

'Oh, look at that cute little boy over there!' she exclaims, catching sight of a toddler in a pushchair. Recently she's been appreciating little children, rating them in terms of adorability rather than mere inconvenience caused. She's not fully conscious of the process herself, but she's beginning to project the image of her own genetic cocktail onto their outlines.

'Hasn't that little boy got lovely hair!' she says.

'If you say so. I prefer the dog.' Russell yawns again, and Mandy hopes he won't inhale as he does so: sometimes she fears disappearing head-first down his gullet.

'Notice anything different?' she prompts gently, tired of waiting for a compliment on her new dyed, bobbed hairstyle. She doesn't see herself as pretty but does her best. Russell doesn't answer her. *You make me feel plain,* she registers sadly, but then perks herself up, entranced by the opportunity to people-watch.

'Why do you always have to be so bloody cheerful?' Russell demands. 'I don't get it.'

'I can't help it. I've got a nice new flat, a job, a cat… and you.' She laughs self-mockingly. Mandy has always had a gift for wilful, determined happiness which flies in the face of reality as experienced by anyone else, but this morning she is feeling the dents and bumps which a year with Russell has inflicted. The three months since they moved into their flat have certainly challenged her near-magical powers of optimism-generation. Mandy pats Russell on the wrist. His expression doesn't change. Then he yawns again. *Somebody remind me why I ever thought your features were pleasingly arranged?* Mandy thinks. He ought to show her the same courtesy as he would a stranger.

'Millions of people travel around the world to do what we're doing,' she says, trying to be upbeat again. 'London in the summer! We're so lucky! And the weather's great! I might even get a tan!'

Russell snorts.

Shaitana hears footsteps. She stops inhaling the stale, brassy air to listen. She has little direct experience of the human world but interprets sounds instinctively. She picks out a brisk, self-possessed, chinking tap. The stilettos speed past; this human won't bother stopping. Shaitana relaxes. The moment hasn't come. How long has she been contained within this space, so dark that light might cause her injury? The world's soundless aspects – time, clouds, sun and stars, daylight and night-time – are beyond her imagining. Birds cawing, engines roaring, dogs barking, human conversations evoke fuzzy blots in her mind, but she can't assess their accuracy.

'Was your bacon nice?' Mandy chirps, putting her arm through Russell's as they leave the café. She's desperate to recapture her early morning buoyancy.

'Not bad.' Russell is marginally less down in the mouth now.

They merge with the cosmopolitan crowd and meander between stalls selling clothing, books, knick-knacks, food. Russell halts to browse through jazz and reggae records. Mandy loathes such music but waits for him with gracious patience.

'I'd like to have a look at those antiques over there,' she says after a good half hour.

'Oh. Must you? Really?'

'I won't be long. Go ahead if you want. I'll catch you up.'

'I'll never find you if we get separated.'

'We've got phones! I'm sure we can find each other.' But Russell follows her, and like a scowling boulder, deposits himself next to the stall.

'I'll be quick,' Mandy says, then feels annoyed with herself.

'I should hope so!' Russell straightens himself into his I'm-about-to-launch-into-a-tirade posture. Mandy knows it well.

'Look at this tat! It's everything I despise: tasteless dust-catchers, the detritus of times which, frankly, I'm glad are over. Horse brasses? Seriously? Weird little porcelain dogs? What a load of pointless old crap!'

Mandy begins to feel the shrivelling inside. Why must he always be so pompous?

'Who in their right mind would want somebody else's old chamber pot? What a bloody rip-off!'

The expression of the stallholder tightens, but there's injury in the man's face as well. 'Steady on, mate!'

Mandy turns away, ashamed, feeling stung on his behalf.

Shaitana hears voices: one light, its clear resonance concealing muddled emotions. The other, gruff, impatient, only just containing itself. The hissing feminine whisper.

'Do you have to be so rude? I hate it when you rant like that.'

'He knows he's a con merchant.'

'No, I don't think he is! Just because you don't like antiques!' A moment passes. 'Oh, look at this! It's so "Arabian Nights"! It's pretty!'

'Do we really need that bit of ethnic-y rubbish?'

'It's like Aladdin's lamp!' The soft voice moves about playfully. 'I'm going to make a wish! If I rub it, will the genie get you into a better mood?'

Shaitana's vessel shifts as Mandy admires its delicate fairy-tale form and lustre.

'We haven't rented a state-of-the art minimalist flat for you to fill it with crap.'

The words are a blur to Shaitana, but their tone awakens her interest. She uncoils a touch, twitching like an evil embryo.

'I'm not going to buy it, but I'm allowed to look.' Mandy suddenly feels a thought bubble up like air through mud: *Why on earth did I move in with you? Why did I even think I liked you?*

Reading her face, Russell frowns. 'Is something wrong?'

'No,' Mandy lies. She's not ready to speak the words aloud. *My self-esteem has never been that great, but do I want to spend the rest of my life handcuffed to your moods?*

Charged as a spring, Shaitana readies herself. Her

vengeful demonic creator sent her to prey on human curiosity. She's intended to be part of an eternal onslaught on virtue and delight, but personally, she's indifferent as to the target.

'Give me that,' the deep voice says.

'Don't snatch!' the high one protests.

There's a lurching, a pitching. A jolting thump. Shaitana is launched against the roof of the vessel. The lid flies off. A jarring metallic clatter, and sunrays shatter the darkness.

'Now look what you've done!' the light voice cries. 'Is it dented? Oh, what a pity!'

One figure is clearer to Shaitana's dazzled vision: the larger one. Shaitana doesn't possess the concepts, but Russell looms above her like a building. She propels herself forwards, outwards, expanding into the world.

Mandy can't process what she's seeing. Where did she come from? The swinging ponytail, the peculiar tasselled satin costume, the gymnastic body bursting out of nowhere, closing in on Russell, who looks like he can't believe his luck. Mandy suspects that infidelity could come easily to him. A few more flakes chip off the weathered remains of her love: Russell looks like a conceited, lustful fool. Suddenly, Mandy notices the viciousness on Shaitana's exquisite face. Miraculously, she foresees silver speeding through the air, slashing, drenching Russell with his own glossy essence. She catches the stench of tumbling intestines. She will never think faster in her life.

'Stop!' she cries. 'You grant wishes, don't you?'

Shaitana freezes, irritated. She can't deny that it's part of her brief.

'Don't kill him,' Mandy commands. 'Just send him somewhere else, and don't let him return.'

Rather sulkily, Shaitana bows. An instant later, the street is a shadow lighter. There's a long moment of disbelief, but then Mandy begins to digest the new reality and walks on. She's going to be sad about Russell, undoubtedly. At some unpinpointable time in the future.

THE LAST KEEPERS OF TIME

Pat Abercromby

We are The last Keepers of Time
knocking at the door you closed.
We hold the memories 'til you understand
who you are.

The coach was travelling overnight at great speed from London to Oxford. The occupants were the old Duke of Aylesbury and his eldest – and now disgraced – daughter, Ann, and their entourage. The infant, only a few days old, was to be given to a wet nurse, the wife of a farmer living deep in the Oxfordshire countryside. The couple would raise the child as their own and would be paid a generous stipend to ensure that the child, a girl, would be well looked after. Never was she to be told who she really was, the offspring of a passionate coupling between the Duke's daughter and the son and heir of the King.

The coachman whipped the horses mercilessly under orders from the Duke to speed up. The sound of his daughter's helpless weeping and the high desperate wail of the hungry infant cradled against her mother's empty breasts was more than he could bear.

Suddenly, three huge black-cloaked apparitions appeared out of the mist and stood in the path of the coach in the rutted, muddy road. The horses reared in terror and veered wildly off the road, straight into a deep and murky pond. The coachman tried desperately to whip the horses back to the edge of the road. The horses screamed, their eyes rolling in panic as their flailing hooves met nothing but sucking mud. There were screams and shouts too from inside the coach as it sank ever deeper into the treacherous, muddy depths. One of the wraith-like figures reached into the coach door which had burst open and pulled out the wailing baby just as with a final shuddering groan, horses and coach were swallowed into the inky blackness.

**

Joan had heard the story of the doomed coach and its occupants retold and embellished with gory details by the old villagers who gathered nightly in the King's Arms pub. She, too, was a regular and had to pass the pond on her way home from her nights out, after gossiping aimlessly and drinking with the handful of younger regulars, losing count of the vodka and Cokes she was knocking back. Fending off the wandering hands of big Tommy Gregory, the local Lothario until, thoroughly fed up with the pointlessness of it all, she would stagger home, just to wake up the next morning with an epic hangover and an empty purse. Too much month at the end of the money, she would mutter, determined to cut back on her drinking, but invariably, boredom would drive her back to the pub the next evening.

Funny, she never did feel scared walking (usually weaving unsteadily) along the road past the pond, even after closing time, despite the dire warnings of Billy Bonkers (as she called him), the town crier.

'Wouldn't catch me walking past that pond at night,' he boomed. 'My family's lived here for generations, that stretch of road is definitely haunted. People have been known to disappear, never to be seen again.'

'Yeah, right, Billy. They were probably drunk and fell into the pond.'

Silly old fool, she thought to herself as she walked unsteadily down the hill. There were no streetlights on this stretch, but this night, a three-quarters Halloween moon shone a silvery pathway ahead of her. She dismissed the noise in her head at first, *Must be imagining this.* But no, there it was, the sound of carriage wheels and horses' hooves. She turned around transfixed, to see a speeding coach and horses bearing down on her. She saw the flaring of the horses' nostrils as the coachman whipped their flanks. She staggered backwards. Her mouth opened in a silent scream. The ground gave way beneath her feet. She was sinking into the slime and mud. Her flailing arms scrabbled desperately for something solid to grasp. Nothing. She sank below the muddy water, mouth and eyes squeezed shut. *Oh God, please no. Not like this.*

The shadowed features of three huge black-cloaked figures loomed over her as she lay, face upwards on the road at the side of the pond. Was this what being dead was like? She felt no fear as one of the wraith-like figures bent lower; all she could make out were the eyes, a strange deep grey, holding her gaze. Inside her head, she heard the words, 'Find who you are.' Her eyes closed.

'Can you hear me? Open your eyes, please! I've called an ambulance, they're on the way. You'll be okay.' The voice was urgent, breathless, the accent unfamiliar.

She opened her eyes and stared, out of focus into the face of a man, his face and body spattered with peaty-smelling muddy slime. She was vaguely aware of a car engine running just behind him, the headlights still on, cutting through the blackness. The sound of the approaching ambulance, siren wailing, blue light flashing in her peripheral vision, washed over her. She tried to speak but choked on the foul-tasting mud in her mouth. Her eyes closed and she sank into oblivion.

***

'Good morning. I'm just going to check your blood pressure.'

Reluctantly, Joan opened her eyes to the early morning bustle on the hospital ward and the friendly open features of the ward sister in her blue uniform.

'You gave the night staff a bit of a challenge trying to wash all that smelly mud off you! The doctor will be round soon to check you over.' She checked the suspended bag, dripping clear fluid through the canula on the back of Joan's hand.

'Antibiotics, just in case you swallowed some nasties from that pond. All being well, you can go home tomorrow.'

It was hard to keep her eyes open. She exhausted but her dreams were weird. She kept seeing a tall, shadowy, black-cloaked figure moving away from her, a faint, half-imagined voice inside her head,

'Find who you are.'

She opened her eyes to find herself looking at the pleasant face of a man, oddly familiar, warm grey eyes crinkling at the corners as he smiled.

'Hi, I'm Charlie, I just came by to see how you are today.'

'Are you – are you the man who…?' Joan's voice trailed off. She could not manage to find the words she wanted.

'Yes, I saw you stumble into that pond last night as I was driving past and pulled you out before you sank out of reach. Quite a fright you gave me, young lady.' He smiled again.

'You… saved me from drowning.' Joan felt tears welling up.

'Think nothing of it. I'll just send you my dry-cleaning bill.' He laughed and pulled out a clean white linen handkerchief from the pocket of his tweed jacket and handed it to her.

She dabbed at her eyes, suddenly enjoying the banter of this stranger with the unfamiliar accent who still used laundered handkerchiefs. 'I'll wash it and get it back to you.'

Charlie came back to visit her in hospital again. She had developed a chest infection and was kept in for a few more days under observation, in case the infection turned into pneumonia. It did not, but it gave them both an opportunity to chat. Gradually, the trauma of her near-death experience faded in the reassuring company of Charlie, who was Canadian, doing his doctorate in Genealogy at Oxford University. She could not understand what pleasure he seemed to get from her company. She had left school with only two GCSEs and one of those was in domestic science. She had a dead-end job with a local firm of estate agents, answering the phone and retrieving sheets of house details for sale or rent from the filing cabinet. And she was always in the pub, drinking too much, spending her money. At 29 years old, no family (both her parents had died within a year of one another) and with no significant relationship, Joan felt that her life was a waste. She had nothing to offer anyone, she thought, and certainly nothing for an attractive academic like Charlie. Still, he wanted to keep in touch with her, they exchanged mobile numbers and he texted her regularly, occasionally driving over from Oxford to take her out to dinner.

Joan was having difficulty sleeping. She had the recurring dream of the tall, black-robed figure, always walking away from her and always the insistent voice in her head: 'Find who you are.' She had told Charlie about the legend of the Duke of Aylesbury and his daughter drowning in the pond, and how the baby was pulled out, just as Charlie had rescued her. She did not tell him about her dreams, that was just too weird.

A few months later, the firm of estate agents she worked for relocated to another town and she lost her job. Joan had no car and the public transport was unreliable. Anyway, Joan thought that they were probably glad of an excuse to get rid of her, she had been frequently late for work, hung-over and unable to concentrate. Oddly, since she had come out of hospital she had stopped going to the pub and only had a glass of wine or two with Charlie when he took her out to dinner.

'Joan, I have a proposition for you,' said Charlie, smiling at her across the restaurant table between them. He leaned over and took her hand.

Joan held her breath, surely not a marriage proposal? She wasn't ready for this; they had not even slept together.

'I need a researcher to help me with my Doctorate. Would you be willing to come and live near me in Oxford? My landlady has another small apartment for rent. I could afford to pay you a wage that would cover your rent, but maybe not enough for anything else. If you could perhaps get another part-time job in Oxford…?' He seemed to run out of steam.

'Are you sure, Charlie? I'm pretty useless you know.' Was he really serious?

'Joan, don't underestimate yourself. You are an amazing woman. You can be anything you want to be.' Charlie squeezed her hand as her eyes misted over. He whipped his laundered handkerchief out of his pocket and handed it to her. This was becoming a habit. 'Is that a "Yes" then?'

Later that evening as he dropped Joan off outside her flat, he said, 'By the way, I checked into the history of the story you told me about the doomed coach. Turns out that the daughter did have a baby to the King's son. They knew it was his because of the large birth mark on the baby's head. Apparently, all the children from that lineage had that same birth mark.' He said it lightly, but stared intently at her.

She did not reply.

'Goodnight Joan. I'll give you a call tomorrow. I can't tell you how pleased I am that you have agreed to come and work for me.' He leaned over and kissed her cheek.

Joan stood in front of her bathroom mirror, pulled her hair back from her forehead looking as she often did, at the edge of the large birthmark just visible under her hairline. She knew Charlie had seen it too, the first time he visited her in hospital.

'The Last Keepers Of Time,' *extract from song lyrics by Kim Abercromby.*

BAD TIMING

Jane MacKinnon

Mrs Newman flipped the sign to 'Closed' and glanced at her watch. Six o'clock. It should have been early closing, but Mrs Carruthers had asked for a late afternoon appointment. The girls would have been home from school for an hour and a half and she should be getting back. They were perfectly capable of making tea for themselves, mind you, so it really didn't matter that she'd be a little late – and it had been well worth staying open. Mrs Carruthers was a good customer and, as President of the Women's Institute, had influence in the local community. It had been important to find and fit the perfect corset for her. Without the right foundation garment, as Mrs Newman repeated time and time again, the most expensive outfit was no better than a jumble sale buy. Mrs Carruthers had been pleased.

'Oh, thank you Mrs Newman, you're such a treasure. You're so, well, reassuring…' Mrs Newman had smiled. She understood exactly what 'reassuring' meant. Mrs Carruthers, like many of her clients, was inclined to stoutness: a tweed-skirted body supported by thick legs and sensible shoes and topped with a tightly permed head of short, grey curls. Mrs Newman herself was, she knew, no oil painting. She, too, had grey hair but rather more femininely styled; her features, though a bit heavy, were carefully made up. Nothing too brash, nothing to frighten the horses as it were. She had a boyish figure (she would have loved more curves) that allowed her to dress smartly but not seductively. Not like the previous manageress who'd had the figure and fashion sense of a chorus girl: long legs and high bosoms that had no need of the engineering feats required by the likes of Mrs Carruthers. That manageress had left in disgrace – and in the company of the local Chairman of the Parish.

No wonder the good womenfolk of the town found Mrs Newman – the decidedly plain Mrs Newman – 'reassuring' and it suited her just fine.

Not all her customers were of the same build. Mrs Newman had a good eye for flattering lingerie and women of all ages came in search of something to make them feel feminine and attractive – lacy baby doll pyjamas, silk nightwear, satin-trimmed housecoats – for honeymoons, romantic dates, illicit affairs. Even husbands came in, awkward at first until she put them at their ease, steering them away from anything that might be deemed too saucy ('Is this what your wife would want to wear? Or is it what you would like her to wear? Let me show you something that you'd both like…') Oh yes, along the way, Mrs Newman had discovered that selling lingerie and matrimonial counselling went hand in hand.

The irony never escaped her.

Now, she stood in the empty shop and, on impulse, took a folded lace nightdress from the shelf. It was part of a new range – beautiful, but a bit expensive. Worth the gamble? She shook it open and felt the delicate fabric slip through her hands. Oh, yes. It would be a winner. She would like to have buried her face in its softness but couldn't risk soiling it with make-up. She would have loved to have taken it for herself, but it was too small. Perhaps she could order a larger size… She stopped the train of thought. Who would she wear it for? Mr Newman was out of reach.

'Oh, David, David, how I miss you.'

She re-folded the pretty wisp of a garment and put it back.

Walking briskly to her Mini – one of the first off the production line and her pride and joy – she brought herself back to reality and reflected on the things that were going well in her life. Getting the job as manageress of a highly respectable lingerie shop was more than she could have hoped for. The position of housekeeper to a widower and his two daughters completed her world. Free accommodation. Her own room, her own bathroom. What more could she want? There was even space for a table and her sewing machine, enabling her to take on private orders for nightgowns and housecoats, frothy diaphanous concoctions of nylon and lace.

As she drove up the hill, she remembered that, some time ago, she had promised to make a housecoat for each of the girls. Her failure to do so, combined with her tardiness this evening gave her a twinge of guilt. The twinge turned into a spasm when she turned into the drive and saw her employer's car – why was he home so early? Typical! The one time she was late back… A black bicycle was propped against the porch. She didn't recognise it, but something gnawed at the back of her mind and she felt uncomfortable. The back door was open. She stepped from a bright outdoors to the muted light of the hallway, taking a moment for her eyes to adjust to the change. Then she saw the chaos. Papers scattered everywhere, the drawers of the hall table open, a suitcase lying on the floor and there, in the middle of the hall rug, her own beloved sewing machine. Burgled. *Oh God,* supposing it had happened when she should have been there? She followed the sound of voices coming from the living room. The older girl was talking; a police officer was taking notes.

'As soon as I opened the door, I knew something wasn't right, but I didn't see the broken window straight away.'

'Well, it looks as if the burglar left in a hurry. Perhaps you surprised him. What time did you say you got home?'

'About half past four.'

'And you didn't see anyone? No one in the garden or running down the drive?'

She shook her head.

The police officer turned to the widower. 'I appreciate that you'll have to check what's missing, but could I ask you to leave all this untouched?' He gestured towards the open drawers and cupboards.

Mrs Newman coughed lightly. 'Surely I can tidy up? You can't expect the family to live in this mess…'

'Thank you, Mrs Newman,' said the widower, 'but I think you should take the evening off. Clearing up will have to wait until tomorrow. They'll have to dust everything for fingerprints, you see.'

Stupidly, Mrs Newman hadn't seen, but now she did. She saw with a clarity that froze her soul and sapped the strength from her body. Kindly arms supported her, lowered her gently into an armchair.

'It's the shock,' said the police officer, knowingly. 'Perhaps one of the girls could put the kettle on.'

Mrs Newman did not take the evening off. While the family went out to a small local restaurant for a meal, she was hard at work, cleaning and polishing every surface. Come eight o'clock, however, she realised she could never finish, had been foolish even to think she could. She'd just wasted time, putting off the inevitable.

She went up to her ransacked room, pushed as many possessions as possible into a large Gladstone bag and hurried downstairs. She had to leave before the family returned. They would imagine, she reasoned, that she had also gone out for the evening. And, as she always left early to open the shop, they wouldn't miss her until the following evening. She cast a final longing glance at her sewing machine, went outside and locked the door. As she climbed into the Mini, she realised with sadness that she would have to sell it, that this might be the last time she would drive it. She had no idea where she was going, just that she had to get as far away as possible. There was no-one she could call, not with David still in prison. Loneliness, once again, would be her companion.

Mrs Newman was right: the family did not remark upon her absence that evening. If anything, they were relieved not to have had to share these hours with someone with whom they had no particular empathy. The widower was tormenting himself for carelessness in leaving so much cash in an unlocked drawer. The older girl was rehearsing the drama she would play before her schoolmates the next day. The younger girl was holding on tightly to her cat, relieved that no harm had befallen it.

With morning, came the excitement of detective work and of having fingerprints taken, each family member rolling thumbs and fingertips across an inky pad and carefully transferring them.

Mrs Newman was not present. 'You will,' they assured the police, 'find her at the lingerie shop.'

But the sign on the lingerie shop door was still turned to 'Closed'.

Mrs Newman had gone.

There was a general leaping to conclusions: house burgled plus housekeeper disappears equals housekeeper guilty.

The widower, a private man, despaired of this common tittle-tattle. 'Do they not appreciate,' he said, 'that Mrs Newman had no need to break the window? She had a key.' But he could not understand why she had run away.

Three days later he understood. How could he have been duped like this? She'd seemed so trustworthy, so reassuring.

The police officer had been polite, even sympathetic (was there a twitch of a smirk?) as he explained the situation. Yes, they had identified the fingerprints of the intruder – a known local ne'er-do-well – and had apprehended him. But.

Such a huge 'but'.

'Other fingerprints have been found,' he said. 'Mrs Newman's fingerprints.'

'Well, of course,' said the widower.

If the constable had summoned a drum roll or produced the words with a flourish from a rabbit-filled top hat, the effect could not have been more astonishing. Mrs Newman was known to the police. Mrs Newman had escaped from the psychiatric ward of a prison. Mrs Newman had been locked up for acts of gross indecency. Mrs Newman is a man.

What were the widower's first thoughts? That his daughters might have been in peril? No, not at all. He was already shrinking at the ribbing that would come from members of his golf club. 'Good God, dear fellow – don't you know what a woman looks like anymore? You need to get out more.'

The older girl was outraged. 'He talked to me about periods!'

The facts were kept from the younger girl.

Not a thought was given to Mrs Newman.

Joanna Newman, known to the police as Joseph Dent, drove north into the night, overwhelmed by fear and panic, not knowing where this journey would end. Please, please not back to the old life of sordid one-night stands, of emotionally barren acts of sex – crude responses to a basic need for human contact. Not back to the awful self-loathing, the constant fear of being caught in some grotty bar or public lavatory.

All that had changed when she met David Newman. He loved her, he let her be the person she really was, he wanted to share her life. Mr and Mrs Newman had settled into a quiet life in rural Gloucestershire.

They never found out which spiteful person had tipped off the police about the queers who lived in the bungalow at the edge of the village. There'd been a small but hostile crowd at their gate when they were arrested and taken away, cries of 'shame' and 'perverts', even rotten fruit thrown at them. They were treated like criminals for, according to the law of the land, they were criminals.

Now, the humiliation, fear and bewilderment were catching up with her again. So often, Joanna wished that she hadn't come into this world as a Joseph; wished, indeed, that she'd never been born – for to be herself was a crime.

***

It would be six long years before she and David could legally share their love. The Sexual Offences Act of 1967 decriminalised homosexual acts in private between consenting men over the age of 21. By then Joanna and David were in their early fifties; it would be decades before society accepted them. Their only crime was to be born at the wrong time.

RECYCLED

Pat Abercromby

I pushed through the dense foliage around the door to my flat on the sixteenth floor. Bathed in the south-facing light from the floor-to-ceiling window, the grapevines, heavy with their luscious bounty hanging low were so tempting. If only I could snatch a bunch, just a small one, for myself — but it was not worth the risk.

There were three other flats on this floor. The lintel around the door directly opposite mine was festooned with hanging baskets of ripe tomatoes. The door on the left was almost invisible under a blanket of green bean vines, growing up a lattice of bamboo stakes, the red bean flowers contrasting with the pale green fuzziness of the developing runner beans. I envied the occupant of the flat on the right. Around that door were low-growing fragrant shrubs of sage, rosemary, thyme and marjoram. Less tempting than the grapes, tomatoes and runner beans. Nevertheless, the red light blinking in the ceiling had all four doors in its sights. At least we were not responsible for keeping our door gardens viable, Central Control in the basement monitored the hydroponic system on all floors including the roof gardens and the greenery, mostly evergreens and small trees growing up the outside of all the high-rise blocks, provided vertical protection against the ravages that climate change had wrought in my lifetime.

***

James McDonald and I had loved one another since we were children. Our two families had been evacuated from our town on the west coast of Scotland. When the rising sea levels of the Atlantic had finally overwhelmed our streets, and our houses were damp from repeated floodings, the Agents from Central Control forced our community to be moved to the higher ground of Inverclachan in the Highlands. I was upset that our grandparents did not come with us but my father said that they did not want to leave their home. I was puzzled because I knew Grandma had said that the Agent had orders to evacuate the whole town. Father got angry and said I was not to talk about them any more. The painful grip on my shoulders as he shook me into silence was enough to scare me into obedience.

As we grew up, James and I spent as much time as we could together until one day, when we were caught outside the Boundary, arms wrapped around one another, the stirrings of new passion spreading through our young, eager bodies, the Agents descended like silent Valkyries dragging us back to the compound. In front of The Assembly that same day, we were shamed and humiliated. Only the chosen ones were allowed to join the breeding programme. James was banished to work permanently on the floating farm on the loch-side to tend the few dairy and beef cattle. He was forced to spend back-breaking hours gathering enough of the scrubby grass left growing in the exhausted soil to feed the cattle. These were intended for the tables of the privileged few, the feared Procurator Fiscal, his Agents and their cohorts from Central Control.

I was sent to work and live in the basement laundry of my building, my punishment for three years. I had to hand wash and wring out the grey towels and bedding from each apartment on a monthly rota. I was only allowed to come out and into the Light for a few hours on Sunday when we all attended a lecture by the head Agent of our sector. He always had a rant about the need to conserve energy: all electric lights were to be turned off by 9pm; personal laundry was to be hand washed only every two weeks; one tepid three-minute shower was allowed only once per week; and all paper, cardboard and food waste was to be recycled.

My bedsit contained a single bed, a small chest of drawers, a fold-up table with one hard-backed wooden chair, a small oven, grill and hotplate, a sink which doubled as a washbasin, a chemical toilet, and a small shower cubicle.

Dominating the back wall by the sink stood three bins. The large one was for recycling paper, cans, cardboard and glass bottles (plastic had been banned years ago) which was emptied monthly by the recycle robots into the recycle chute in the central atrium, and went down to the basement. Here more recycle robots separated it all out before it was sent to the recycling plant which stood in the middle of our six greenery-clad high-rise buildings.

The second smaller one was for food waste and was collected weekly by a specialist robot which macerated the contents of the food bins right there in our rooms and emptied the resulting slush into a trolley which it pulled along. This was destined to be mixed with the slurry from the cow farm and turned into fertiliser for the crops. Each sector had to be self-sufficient in food production so producing good quality fertiliser was vital to our crop yield.

The third, general waste bin was smaller still and often an Agent would enter the room without warning (we were not allowed to lock the doors) and tip the contents onto the floor, checking that nothing recyclable had been thrown out. Even the discovery of a potato peel would result in the harsh punishment of a week on half-rations. Only water and a thin watery stew would be allowed. This was agonising when on my floor, the tantalising grapes and tomatoes were right in front of our noses.

My neighbours were all in their fourth decade like me, three women and one man. On one occasion, an Agent silently entered one of the bedsits and found a man and woman making love on the single bed. They were taken away and we never saw them again. The rumour was that they had been sent to the Central Recycling Sector. Nobody knew exactly what happened there, but we were all scared of the many stories and rumours that circulated, rushing through each sector like malevolent Chinese whispers.

At first, I had lived with my parents in a one-bedroomed apartment on the third level of this high-rise building, but when I was released from my basement punishment in the steamy, rancid laundry room after three years, my parents were gone. They had been removed, I was told, to 'another sector' for older residents. I never found out where they had gone. I was moved into this bedsit on the sixteenth level twenty-one years ago and given the task of cleaning the solar panels on the roof. I brushed away the dropped leaves and bird mess left by the flocks of screeching seagulls that now outnumbered the songbirds from the dwindling hedgerows and fields.

From up on the roof, I could see between the gaps of the six high-rise buildings in our sector, to where the floating cattle farm bobbed at the edge of the loch. Occasionally, I thought I caught a glimpse of James's broad shoulders and bright hair as he moved around the cow stalls, and my heart would leap.

One day when I was brushing the leaves off one of the solar panels on the roof, I found a torch that the maintenance engineer must have dropped. With racing pulse, I shoved it deep into the pocket of my brown uniform and by accessing the intranet in our building, I was able to learn the basics of Morse code. I learned the code for 'Jamie', my pet name for him when we were young, and any time I saw James on the floating cattle farm I flashed the torch on and off to signal him with my message. For weeks nothing happened until at last, I saw an answering flash of light from the cattle farm. Dit dit dit, dot dot dot. It didn't mean anything, but I knew James had seen my torch flashing. He must have found a way to learn Morse code as I had, because eventually I could make out his message: 'boundary'. Meeting at the Boundary was very risky as the Agents patrolled the perimeter fence after dark with powerful flashlights. I crept down the stairs of the central atrium, not wanting to meet an Agent in the lift. But on this night, my guardian angel must have been with me as I reached the Boundary without being stopped. James suddenly appeared out of the gloom and pushed me back into the shadow of the fence.

'Grace, I can't believe it's really you. It has been so long,' he whispered and pulled me close. His body had changed, he was broad and muscular from the hard, physical work, but his voice was still the same. The soft burr of our home-town accent and the sweet, fresh sweat smell of his skin was intoxicating.

'Oh Jamie,' I whispered back. 'I thought I would never see you again. I am so glad you saw my torchlight.'

The years since we had last seen one another melted away as we stood in our tight embrace.

'Come with me, Grace. I know a safe place where we can talk.'

He led me along the fence, both crouching low, until, with a soft push, a fence panel yielded, and we squeezed through. We were on the outside! We ran, I was stumbling but steadied by Jamie's firm hold on my hand. We were headed straight for a small copse of oak trees. Quite suddenly, we were enfolded in leafy security, the canopy of the overhead branches filtering tiny fingers of starlight onto my upturned face. My dear Jamie, weather-beaten and aged, his bright hair streaked with silver but still looking at me with eyes full of love. I rarely ever looked at myself in a mirror, but I knew that my face and my hair also showed signs of the hard time we had both had trying to survive in the harsh regime of our sector. We were not among the young people who were selected for the breeding programme and were fed better rations; we unlucky ones, the workers, lived on meagre fare. That we were now so much older did not matter to

Jamie or me.

Jamie and I lay together all that night on the leafy, loamy forest floor, only creeping back to our quarters before dawn broke. For the first time since we had been forced to leave our coastal home when I was a young girl, I experienced an inner contentment that I can only think was happiness. We did not dare meet that way very often, it was too dangerous, but when we did risk it, the partings became more and more painful to endure.

'Somehow, I will find a way to get us out of here, Grace. If we can make it to the open sea at the far end of the loch, perhaps we can find a ship to take us to America.' He was so earnest and I loved him all the more for it. 'I have been collecting large pieces of driftwood and have started building a raft. I keep it hidden under the floating farm but we might have to wait for a while until I can finish it. I need more wood.'

I didn't dare tell him we had no time to wait. I knew by now that I was pregnant and when my condition became obvious to the Agents, I would be hauled up before the Procurator Fiscal. I knew what my punishment would be, it was a capital offence for a woman who was not selected for the breeding programme to become pregnant and also for the man if he got caught.

I concealed my pregnancy from Jamie for as long as possible, determined to protect him at all costs, but as soon as he found out, he was demented with worry for me and the baby.

'Oh God, Grace! What have I done! I must get you away from here before they suspect that you are pregnant.'

I did everything I could to disguise my growing stomach by wearing bigger sizes of the ugly brown tunics and trousers. One windy day when I was about seven months gone, I was sweeping leaves off a solar panel when one of the maintenance men appeared. The wind had masked the noise of him opening the door onto the roof, taking me by surprise and I had no time to adjust my tunic which the wind had flattened against my body. I saw him looking at me, a sly smile on his mean little face. He had never liked me since I had been given this job years ago. He was always muttering under his breath that his wife, who worked in the dank basement laundry room deserved to be doing my job 'in the Light'. I could hardly breathe for the panic that flooded my body and my baby kicked in protest. He disappeared back down the stairs without saying a word. I just had time to flash an SOS with my torch, praying that Jamie might see it, before two Agents burst onto the roof and roughly dragged me to the lift. There was no point pleading for mercy, there was none to be had.

My trial was short and terrifying. I was brought before the Procurator Fiscal in the Assembly Hall. All the residents of our sector were there to witness the sentence passed on me. The Agents had done their best to make me confess who the father of my baby was, but I refused to tell them. I knew Jamie would be in the Hall and I prayed that he would not reveal himself as my lover. Fortunately, most of the bruises and cuts from the whippings were on my back and legs, concealed by my brown uniform. The female Agent who was assigned to make me confess, had, for some reason, avoided whipping my stomach. I soon found out why.

The Procurator Fiscal in his black and purple robes was flanked by twelve Agents, six on each side on the raised podium. The Agents were clad in the dress tartans of their Clans. Dimly, I noted that the only Agent who was not glaring triumphantly at me was the one wearing the Campbell tartan, my own Clan's green and black colours. His eyes were cast downwards, staring at the floor.

The Procurator Fiscal noisily cleared his throat.

'Grace Campbell, you have committed a capital offence by becoming pregnant and there is only one punishment that this sector can pass. Your baby, however, is an innocent party in this heinous crime against your community. You will be confined to prison for a further eight weeks and the child will be removed from your body at thirty-six weeks. Thereafter, you will be taken to the Central Recycling Sector for immediate disposal.'

He brought his black, silver encrusted gavel down hard on the table in front of him, stared hard at me for a few seconds, turned and swept out of the Assembly Hall, his black and purple gown flowing behind him.

'This is for the brat you are carrying.' The Agent slapped a bowl with hot porridge on the rough-hewn table in my windowless cell. 'Consider yourself lucky, at least you will get fed until your bairn is removed.'

The cells were in the basement, lit only by the weak shafts of light that reached through the bars from the roof window of the central atrium far above. The days were growing shorter as the hot season morphed into the cooler weather after the Equinox.

The long nights were the worst. When daylight faded, the blackness descended like a thick cloak. It was impossible even to see my hand in front of my face. There was little comfort for my swelling body or my tortured mind as the days ticked by towards the end. All I could be grateful for was that our baby would be saved and that Jamie might one day escape from this place when his raft was built.

At least once during the endless hours of night, the duty Agent would complete his patrol by shining a flashlight into my cell, presumably to check that I was still alive. I was oddly comforted by this nightly intrusion into the black void that was my reality. It was the only reminder that my baby, now kicking vigorously against my tight abdomen, and I, were not totally abandoned.

I could tell by my size that I must be close to the thirty-sixth week of my pregnancy. My terror and despair had dulled into a helpless, hopeless acceptance of what was to come. I just wanted it to be over. I did manage to swallow down the porridge and the small portions of chicken and vegetables that were thrust into my cell twice a day, to give the baby a chance to survive the trauma of being ripped from my body too early. Another black night descended and I lay down to count the slow intakes of my breath, my only connection with my stubborn heart that kept on beating.

This time the light from the torch swept over me repeatedly until reluctantly, I was forced to open my eyes. The whispered voice was urgent.

'Get up, lass, and come with me.'

I was flooded with fear. Was this it? Had my time

come? A rough-skinned hand pulled me to my feet and I was half dragged through the door of my cell. I had no choice but to hold on to the man's hand as I was propelled through the impenetrable blackness. We stopped abruptly and I saw the faint light of his torch switched on to illuminate the outlines of a heavy studded, wooden door. I heard the key turn and the door, creaking ominously on its hinges, swung open. The cool night air shocked my body into sudden alertness. What was happening? The waning moon, so long hidden from me, lit up the face of my captor. It was my Clansman, the one Agent who had not looked at me when I was sentenced. A Campbell.

'James is waiting for you at the Boundary. Go quickly, don't look back.'

I had no time to thank him. He had thrust the torch into my hand and evaporated into the shadow of the building.

I stumbled towards the Boundary fence, my breath rasping and laboured as the heaviness of my body and the weakness in my leg muscles pitched me forward. I dared not use the torch and was guided only by the faint beams of the moon. I was sure that at any moment the sweeping flashlight from a patrolling Agent would catch me in flight. I was within a metre of the Boundary when I saw the Agent's flashlight. I froze. I was quickly pushed to the ground. It was Jamie. He covered my body with his. The high whine of the siren cut through the silence. Neither of us breathed. We heard the sound of the Agent's boots running back towards the sector, the beam of his flashlight frantically sweeping wide arcs across the building.

The water of the loch was cold but calm as Jamie lifted me onto his raft and we pushed away from the hidden mooring underneath the floating farm. We both had a makeshift paddle and despite the raft tipping precariously, we finally made it to the opposite shore – a wild, uninhabited area of dense woodland. Jamie hauled the raft ashore and dragged it into the undergrowth. The backpack of provisions that he had strapped to the raft had survived the crossing.

We stood facing one another, hands locked in a tight grip.

'Grace, this is our only chance. Will you trust me to keep you and our baby safe?'

'Yes, Jamie, always.'

He took my hand, hefted the backpack onto his shoulder and led us deeper into the woods.

***

As dawn broke over the sector, Agent Campbell took his last look at the red-streaked sky before his weary body was pushed through the door of the Central Recycling Sector. He was at peace. His sacrifice was worth this price. His promise to Grace's father had been kept, and the honour of his Clan upheld.

SEAT 18A

Charlene K. Haar and Elizabeth A. Prais

'Have you noticed the man with the dried blood where his ear should be?' I gently nudged my neighbour in Seat 18A with my left elbow and mouthed, using my eyes to direct his attention to the seat in front and to my right.

The young man looked up from his phone. During the brief conversation when he arrived in our row, I learned he had been on a business trip but managed to catch an early flight home. Pleasantries over, he had dived into his phone to answer his emails.

I watched him scrutinise the row in front of us then his eyes flicked back to mine.

'Another one – sitting on the aisle,' he mouthed back, his chin jutting towards the other side of the plane.

Slowly turning in my seat, I felt a flutter of apprehension in my stomach. My seat mate was correct; across the aisle in the row in front of us sat another man with bloody patches on his face and neck and no ear.

The appearance of my friend Sandy sliding into the empty seat next to mine startled me. She immediately opened up the guidebook to one of the pages she had tabbed and started reciting plans for our long weekend, after explaining that the cabin crew said she could move once the doors had closed. My mind was so full of thoughts I couldn't follow what she was saying.

Sandy sensed my distress and laid a hand on my arm. 'You okay?'

I gave a curt nod towards the man on the aisle; I could see him over her right shoulder. Sandy still had a smile on her face as her head turned right. The smile was gone when she turned back to me; her eyes were wide and her mouth had dropped open.

'Another one,' I mouthed while pointing to the seat in front of her and then held up two fingers.

A small gasp escaped from Sandy and her eyes opened wider still.

'There is a little boy with each of them.'

She leaned in towards me, her mouth near my ear.

'Has the cabin crew noticed?'

I shrugged my shoulders and shook my head.

'I think we should say something before we take off. If they are on the run it will be better if it's dealt with here…' Her arm moved up to hit the call button.

The captain's announcement filled the cabin with calm, measured words telling us all that the plane had been allocated a slightly earlier slot; we should all fasten our seatbelts as our departure had been moved up.

While the rest of the cabin buzzed with the news Sandy and I looked at each other with clenched jaws. She lowered her arm.

'Here comes the flight attendant!' Sandy whispered excitedly. We held our breaths as a flight attendant, still with a deflated life jacket around her neck, scanned each row slowly ensuring all bags were safely stowed, tray tables were up and seatbelts on.

She passed row 17 with no comment.

The flight attendant looked directly at me. 'Your bag,' she pointed to my handbag sitting on my lap, 'needs to be under the seat in front of you.' She gave me a small smile, waiting for me to comply before moving on.

'Why didn't you say anything?' asked Sandy with exasperation.

I shrugged my shoulders sheepishly.

Sandy squeezed my arm and rolled her eyes while she quickly dug out her notebook and pen, replacing her bag before an attendant spotted her.

As soon as her notebook was out Sandy started scribbling messages:

Could these men be fathers to the boys? Then:

Do you think the men are related... one is definitely older...

Can the flight attendants ask about the safety of the children?

Should we start a conversation with the boys?

I'm looking at the knuckles of the men... there doesn't appear to be any damage to their hands... what could have happened to their ears??

Why wouldn't they at least clean up so that there would be less dried blood around the places where their ears used to be?

Could a fight with brass knuckles have done something like that?

Could this be an example of child trafficking? What shall we do? What CAN we do?

Did you know that Russia and the Ukraine were well

known for trafficking?

Portugal has a reputation for trafficking of men, women AND children?

After a moment thinking, Sandy's eyes lit up. 'Cage fighters!' she whispered to me excitedly before opening up her phone and logging into the plane Wi-Fi. Soon she was showing me a video of children as young as six being primed by men to prepare to fight before an audience of screaming and shouting families and fans. The intention was to hurt the other with fists, elbows, arms, knees and legs – all to encourage the development of 'real boys'. Another video showed older men engaged in Mixed Martial Arts.

For the next hour Sandy and I were locked in focused conversation. My seat mate in 18A was long forgotten.

The announcement from the cockpit about our descent into Schiphol took us both by surprise; we weren't ready. The landing gear doors were opening and we still had no plan.

'Right!' I swallowed hard and decided to take charge of the situation. 'When they get up, take a good look at the man and boy across the aisle. I'll do the same for the people on this side. We'll find a guard and tell them.'

Sandy nodded and gave me a quick thumbs up.

The aircraft had come to stop at the gate but the occupants of row 17 were slow to move, waiting until the rows ahead emptied. The man on our side of the plane was hesitant to stand, his hand rested on his back when he did. Reaching up to pull down his carry-on he let out a groan before taking the hand of the little boy.

5'11", brown hair, brown eyes, red polo shirt, jeans, mid-30s.

I repeated the description to myself as Sandy and I walked up the air bridge.

My heart was thumping in my chest as we passed through the airport still behind the man/boy pairs. They went through Passport Control well ahead of us.

'How can no one notice?' questioned Sandy as we approached them at the baggage carousel.

'Where are the airport police? Do you think a border patrol will be good enough?' I wondered aloud as Sandy headed off to the far side of the room.

The man who was sitting in seat 18A came up to me.

'Good flight? You and your friend seemed concerned about something.'

'It's just those men, the ones with missing ears. They have two boys with them, and no one seems to notice.'

'You and your friend should have a good weekend and not worry any more about them. I can assure you, plenty of people have noticed.' He gave me a reassuring smile. 'I think your friend is trying to get your attention.' He nodded while looking towards the back wall of the room.

I turned to see Sandy frantically waving at me. I motioned for her to come back to the baggage carousel.

'I found a guard on his way into the loo. I'm sure we can corner him when he comes out,' she replied excitedly.

'My seat mate says not to worry.' I smiled and

turned around fully expecting to see the man from seat 18A and get further explanation. But we would never hear the rest of the story.

I looked around the baggage area and they were all hurriedly walking away together: the man from Seat 18A, the men with missing ears and the two small boys.

Based on true events!

A CLASS ACT

Jane MacKinnon

Her eyes they shone like diamonds
You'd think she was the queen of the land
Her hair hung over her shoulder
Tied up with a black velvet band

The lilting tale of flirtation filled the chalet room. In the corner, a wood-burning stove flickered with warmth while, outside, the snow sparkled in the light from the windows. He was perched on a tall stool at the kitchen bar, his head nodding in time to the music, his eyes half closed so that he could study the girl. She was still dressed for work: a modest black skirt, white tee-shirt, hair neatly tied back. She looked classy, he thought – and very, very pretty. What did she see in him? He couldn't believe his luck.

'There's something cosy about folk songs, don't you think?' said the girl with just a hint of an Irish lilt. 'They make me feel at home.' Then, 'The skiing should be good tomorrow. Where shall we go?'

His thoughts were elsewhere. 'The blokes must have thrown themselves at you,' he said and immediately wished he hadn't.

But she just shook her head. 'Sure, they were only interested in the chalet girls. I thought working in a bar at a Swiss resort would be a passport to pleasure, but I've never been so knackered in my life. I'd crash out as soon as the clearing up was done and then, when I opened my eyes, it was time to start all over again. So – how lucky am I to find you now! Contract finished and loads of time to have fun and get to know each other!'

She smiled and he liked the way her eyes crinkled at the corners.

'Let me show off my newly-acquired skills,' she said, 'and get you a drink.'

She took a couple of glasses from the cupboard behind her and went across to the fridge. With a flourish and a soft 'pop!' the bottle was opened and she began to pour.

'*Her eyes they shone like diamonds*,' sang the Irish folk band.

He watched the champagne bubble silkily into each glass, poured carefully with no risk of wasteful foaming up and over-spilling.

'My – you've got a steady hand.' He noticed that her hands were smooth and well-manicured and he could imagine their steady, smooth caress.

'Sure, you need one when you're dealing with something – and someone – as special as this.'

He felt like a prince.

'*You'd think she was queen of the land.*'

She placed the glasses on the bar and uncapped the Guinness. Then, oh so slowly, she slid the black liquid on to the surface of the champagne. He watched mesmerised, feeling her concentration, hardly daring to breathe.

'*Her hair hung over her shoulder.*'

She put the bottle aside and held up a glass in triumph. 'And there you have it – Black Velvet!'

At the top of the glass, a crown of dense, creamy foam floated on the dark, opaque Guinness. At the bottom of the glass, the champagne kept its straw-coloured brightness. And where the bitter met the sweet, there was a golden band.

'Here you are – try this!' She passed the glass to him, her fingers lightly brushing his.

He sipped and relaxed with pleasure.

'*Tied up with a black velvet band.*' The chorus finished for the fifth and final time.

He leant across, undid *her* velvet bow and set her blonde hair free.

Much later ('Well, we can't leave an opened bottle of champagne,' she'd reasoned) she told him the origins of the drink. 'It's out of respect for Prince Albert. Everyone and everything had to wear black after he died. Black Velvet is champagne in mourning.'

'Well, aren't you a little mine of information,' he teased, but he was impressed and snuggled into her knowledge.

'There's a poor man's version,' she continued, 'using cider and stout, but I feel that's cheating – and I wouldn't want to cheat you. Not now that we'll be meeting up back in England.'

He snuggled deeper, already imagining them together, choosing a bright golden band with a fair amount of added sparkle.

They talked at length about their reunion. She was flying out of Zurich a couple of days before him, couldn't wait for the two days to pass…

'I'll ring you as soon as I'm home, the very moment I walk through the front door,' he promised.

'No,' she insisted. 'Sooner than that. Just as soon as you're out of the airport.'

On their last night together, she seemed anxious. 'I don't want to leave you,' she said fretfully. Then later, 'Can I ask you something?' She was running her finger round his lips, down his neck, down to the flat of his stomach.

'Of course.' *Anything*, would have been a more accurate response.

'I've bought a necklace for my mammy. It's in a really nice box with a velvet lining and everything, but my bag's so stuffed I can't get it in without crushing it. I could just leave the box behind but it seems a pity. Or… I wondered if… Say if it's not okay, but do you have any room in your case?'

It wasn't a question he'd been expecting but it guaranteed that he really would see her again and he liked the idea of being involved with her family. 'Oh, I'm sure I've got space – of course I'll take it.'

'You're such a sweet man. I'm so lucky.' She gave him a quick kiss and then jumped up to fetch a flat rectangular box, wrapped in gold tissue paper and done up with black velvet ribbon.

'It looks very classy,' he observed.

'Would you like to see it? Or can you wait until Mammy opens it?'

'Oh no, don't unwrap it. It looks too lovely.'

'Presentation is everything,' she smiled.

She kissed him again and crossed the room to the fridge. 'Now – how about a celebratory drink and a toast to our future? It'll be the poor man's version, I'm afraid. I spent my last francs on the necklace.'

'Rich man or poor man, I don't mind,' he laughed.

He didn't laugh two days later when, at the airport, a golden retriever with a black leather collar paid very special attention to his luggage. He was arrested for possession of Class A drugs…

Before the judge and jury, next morning I had to appear.
The judge he says to me: 'Young man, your case is proven clear.
We'll give you seven years penal servitude, to be spent far away
    from the land,
far away from your friends and relations, betrayed by the black
    velvet band.'

THE RELIABLE WITNESS

Sarah-Jane Reeve

Working in a restaurant wasn't how I'm supposed to be spending my gap year, you know. I had some backpacking in mind. I was going with two friends, but would you believe they pulled out at the last minute? So annoying! So, my trip to the Far East has been delayed until I can find someone else to go with. The people are nice here but as a job it manages to be either hectic *or* boring. And life here isn't exactly Instagrammable. I find myself day dreaming about excitement and travel. But Joe the barista and I try to have a laugh.

Bob always comes in at the same time every day. He's only a large homely man in an old raincoat over his suit, about 50. He's one of our regulars. Same time, same meal, every day. We play a game, me and the kitchen staff, to see how quickly we can get his chicken and mushroom panini on the table. If we get it down to under five minutes Bob gives us a tip. Well, it passes the time. That's what passes for entertainment round here.

'Excuse me, is this seat taken?' asked Bob.

The restaurant at lunchtime was packed as usual and it was a hot day. There were only one or two seats left, and Bob made a beeline for the seat next to a young woman in a maroon-coloured hijab.

'Do you mind?' prompted Bob as the woman hadn't said anything. He's ever so polite, most people would have just plonked themselves down.

'It's OK,' said the woman at last. She was shy and kept looking down into her coffee mug. She looked quite nervous.

I started to squeeze my way through the tables towards them, but Bob caught my eye before I got across and just said, 'My usual, Tasha – and a cappuccino.'

He peeled off his raincoat, loosened his tie, sat down, opened his briefcase and took out some papers.

After taking more orders I made my way to Bob's table with his cappuccino, and we joked about not playing our game today because he could see we were frantic. Then the woman in the headscarf picked up her menu and pointed to an item and said something like 'Number 23' in an accent.

'Sorry?' I said.

'Vegetable soup, it's Number 23, I think, Tasha,' said Bob. 'I don't think the lady's from round here.'

'Well, none of us are from round here, are we?' I said. 'It's King's Cross.'

The woman took out her purse and pulled out a bunch of £50 notes.

'OK?' she said.

'More than enough,' I said scribbling on my pad, 'but put that away, we'll sort it out when you've finished.'

As I walked away she was asking Bob about where she could find a bureau de change.

I was really busy for ten minutes with Table 3's order but when I took over Bob's panini and the vegetable soup, I noticed Bob was doing some calculations with her on a piece of paper. She was concentrating so hard that at first she didn't see me standing there with her soup. I had to clear my throat politely. As she finally looked up, I noticed her face was shiny. She had an anorak on, zipped right up to her chin and a long skirt. A bit much for such a warm spring day. I hung up Bob's raincoat for him.

'Can I hang up your coat for you?' I asked her.

But she refused quite abruptly. *Suit yourself,* I thought.

That's when she dropped her menu, and I noticed it. As I picked it up, I saw a wire. It was a loop trailing out below the hem of her jacket. Earphones perhaps? But then Pam, the manager, waved to me saying that Table 4 needed menus.

Later, as I stood at the counter waiting for Joe to make some expressos, I looked back at Bob and the woman and I couldn't help feeling that there was something odd about her. They seemed deep in conversation as if he was explaining something to her. I guessed that he was probably still helping her with the money-changing issue, she was holding something which looked like a passport. She was still clutching the collar of the anorak and as I looked at it closely it seemed too big for her. She kept looking towards the door. Then very slowly, like she didn't want anyone to notice, she took a backpack out from under the table and put it on her lap. And then it hit me – foreigner, wires, backpacks, anoraks, all those suicide bombers on the news. They all looked like that.

My heart started pounding and I looked around for Pam. Where was the manager when you really needed her? I grabbed Joe, and tried to explain that there was something odd about the woman.

'I think she might have a bomb,' I said.

It was as if the next part happened in slow motion. Joe's mouth had just formed an incredulous 'O' shape, when Bob leapt to his feet and shouted something at anorak woman. The chatter in the room died away.

'He's realised – he knows!' I grabbed Joe's arm in terror.

Then the woman reached inside her coat and got to her feet slowly, but for a moment her eyes locked on mine. Then she put out her hand as if she was warning me away. I wanted to run, but I was frozen to the spot.

Then, just as Bob was staggering backwards away from the table, two police officers walked through the door and as he turned, they grabbed him. Then she pulled out something that looked like a badge. She said something calmly but seriously to Bob, and I just caught the end of it: '…anything you do say may be given in evidence.'

'She's police…' I said to Joe.

'Not a bomber then, you idiot! You nearly gave me a heart attack,' said Joe.

Then it all kicked off. Bob's face contorted and he

swore and struggled. He was not like our Bob at all. One of the police officers took handcuffs from the backpack and put them on him.

The other police officer said to the woman: 'Did you get it?'

She nodded and they all smiled. I thought they were going to do a high five but they kept their cool and stayed dignified police officers. Then she took off her anorak and they unhooked what looked like a large phone from around her neck and they hustled Bob out of the door.

Pam walked over to her and the policewoman explained something and then she walked over to me.

'I'm D.S. Nazir. I saw you realising what was happening – I'm so glad you didn't say anything.'

'But Bob…?'

'He's been known to us for a while – fraud – but we couldn't prove it. He's been preying on newcomers to the country and I was very keen to get a recording of him as evidence. Today we finally did it.'

'Bob? I can't believe it – he's one of our regulars…' I babbled. I felt like such a numpty because my mobile was in my locker and I hadn't caught it on video. Of course, Joe was putting it on his Instagram story there and then.

'I wished I'd filmed it,' I said to the D.S. 'It might have helped you.'

'No need, you *saw* it, you're a reliable witness, and that's what we need. Well, thank you for staying calm amongst all the drama – we'll take a statement from you soon.'

2. Unlucky In Love

4 O'CLOCK SHOES

Louise Norton

Hot date at the midnight bar, looking good I thought
    to interest you.
Watching the door and my wristwatch too. Hey, he's
    only a little late…
I'll just recline with my wine.

Ten minutes disappear and he's not here, feeling
    uneasy, all alone.
C'mon baby, pick up the phone, one more sip and I'll
    be fine.
I'll just recline with my wine.

Starting to hate you now, still waiting for you now…
    all alone with empty bottles and painted promises.
I'll just recline with my wine.

Last to leave the bar on my own, only the street to see
    me home.
That seems to dance a different song from me –
    now I'm falling off my 4 o'clock shoes…

And, it's all because of you.

ALL WRAPPED UP IN YOU

Louise Norton

I trace your face in my mind
and I remember
cold air glistening in the wintry sun
all wrapped up in you.

Neon lights glowing nectarine,
sirens dancing to a tambourine;
tightly tango into the night
losing ourselves in the pale moonlight.

Sweethearts racing, kisses on the run,
laughing all the way.
Ice diamonds dazzle to the chimes of your charm
all wrapped up in you.

I trace your face in my mind
and I remember…

Lyrics from the E.P. 'All wrapped up' by Norton and Stutterheim
In memory of Dave.

EMPTINESS

Moyra Zaman

The morning woke without a smile.
He contrived a frown.
She bit her lip.

Their hearts loitered heavily on the bed
as the sun began to scar the day.

Wounds concealed and silently dressed,
she re-entered the world, stage right,
performed to applause, frenetically engaged,
ticking the boxes of her day.

At the last curtain call,
when 'happy hour' had lost its charm,
she returned, alone,
to the sound of 'one hand clapping'.

CRUSHED

Pat Abercromby

'Please, Mum! Everybody at school has a smartphone. Please!'

Amy chose her moment. Her mum was usually tired and grumpy in the mornings. She worked three evenings a week at the pub, in addition to her day job as a secretary at a local firm of chartered accountants. On Saturday mornings her mum had a well-deserved lie-in and stayed in bed reading until 9 a.m. Amy had taken her a cup of tea and a digestive biscuit. Her mum didn't eat breakfast.

'Amy have you any idea how much those things cost? Even the cheapest is about £150 and then there's the contract to consider. If your lazy snake of a father would just get himself a job…'

Here we go again, thought Amy. Another well-worn tirade against her dad who had left them when Amy was eleven to 'take up' with another woman at the other end of town.

'And,' her mother ranted on, 'if he would pay some child support for you, I wouldn't have to knock my pan out at the pub to make ends meet.'

This wasn't going well but she had to take the risk. 'But Mum, I'm fifteen now and I can get a Saturday job. Mr Rashid at the corner shop says I can work there Saturday mornings if I want to and anyway,' she hesitated, 'Dad said he would pay for the contract – so we can keep in touch.'

'Oh yeah? Don't believe a word that comes out of his mouth. What kind of father deserts his wife and child for a tart! Anyway, you see him every other weekend. I don't know how you can stand being in the same house as that floozie of his. Your choice, not mine.'

Amy sat quietly on the edge of her mum's bed, trying not to stress as the diatribe against her dad continued. Then, as often happened, when it was over, her mum's mood softened. She put her hand on her daughter's knee.

'Look, if you can get Mr Rashid to pay you the minimum wage and you agree to pay me back in weekly instalments, I'll get you a smartphone out of the Argos catalogue. At that price I'll get six months interest-free credit to clear my account. Particularly as your useless father said he would cough up for the contract.'

'Thanks, Mum! You're a legend.' She quickly hugged her mum and dashed out of the room to tell Mr Rashid she would take the job, before her mum had a change of heart.

Amy didn't mind spending every other weekend with her dad. She quite liked his partner, call-me-Tracy, I-always-wanted-a-daughter – although she overdid the wanting to be 'best friends' bit with Amy. But the real attraction was her 17-year-old son Kevin, or Kev, as everyone called him. Amy had nursed a massive crush on Kev ever since she had first met him when she was eleven. He rarely took any notice of her, spending most of his time up in his bedroom, whooping and yelling with excitement or frustration as he played some online video game tournament with other internet users. Amy was quite shocked that he used such bad language, but he never swore in front of his mum or her dad.

Kev had left school at sixteen and was now an apprentice motor mechanic. Amy longed for the short time he hung around the kitchen when he came home from his Saturday shift at the garage, hoovering down whatever food his mum had left out for him. His nails were grimed with dirt and he smelt of sump oil, but Amy still adored him. If only he would notice her. But he remained oblivious to her presence in the house. Even when he'd still been at school, hanging around with his mates, all hunched over their smart phones at morning and afternoon breaks, he never acknowledged Amy. She was obviously invisible to him.

The real reason she was so desperate to get a smartphone was so that she could open up a free account on Snapchat like all the other kids at school. She hoped she'd find a find a way to get Kev to message her or to join his group of contacts so she could see what he was doing. She was able to use her Snapchat account to join a group from her class although she rarely bothered to post any messages in case she was ridiculed.

Sally-Anne Herbertson was the most popular girl in Amy's class and outside in the playground too. She was always surrounded by her favourites, a bunch of girls who moved around together like an amoeba throughout the school day. More recently, Amy noticed that she was flirting with the sixth form boys too, who hovered round her like demented moths. Blonde and pretty with her short skirts and her blouse opened one button too low showing the swell of her breasts, was her modus operandi and it seemed to work.

On Friday evenings Amy had the house to herself as her mother worked her evening shift at the pub. On the weekends that she was due to spend with her dad, she would spend ages getting ready to make an impression on Kev. She would wash her unruly long curly hair with shampoo and conditioner from the cheap bulky bottles with foreign labels, that her mother bought from the Pound Store. Her hair would feel shiny and clean, showing up the natural copper tones, but she wished it didn't smell of apples and dishwasher liquid. Amy's hair refused to grow very long; it grew out into a massive bush of curls until, frustrated, Amy would beg a tenner from her mum to get it trimmed back to a more manageable shape. She longed for a salon cut like Sally-Anne was allowed, her long silken hair straightened into a flowing blonde mane.

Amy would sneak into her mother's bedroom and try on her clothes in front of the full-length mirror, twisting her head to try and see her back view. Did her jeans still make her bottom look too big? They did. In despair she would shrug herself into an older stretchier pair, almost transparent at the knees. With a little effort, she could create rips at the knees like the designer jeans a lot of the girls were wearing. Who could tell the difference? She wished she didn't have to wear the ugly glasses. Short-sighted *and* fat at fifteen. It wasn't fair. She found some solace in the left-over shepherd's pie in the plastic container that her mum had heated up in the microwave before she rushed off to work at the pub. Then there was the half raspberry trifle with the thick synthetic cream that was her mum's favourite 'dessert', as she called it.

She had survived another ghastly day at school that Friday. After the lunch break, Sally-Anne had pushed past her in the school corridor, her twittering, sniggering group hard on her heels as usual. Amy thought she heard the words 'fatso' and 'four-eyes'. Her face flamed with embarrassment and her stomach tightened. Did she have time to dash to toilet block? The afternoon classes would be starting soon. She would have to hurry.

Later that night – and before her mother came home – she tried some make-up that her mum had left spilling carelessly out of her make-up bag on the white dressing table. The pink lipstick was a lot darker than the one that Sally-Anne was wearing when she posted her provocative photos on Snapchat. Sleek blonde hair tossed back over one bare shoulder and her full lips pouting like a model. Amy practised the look as best she could and went to bed.

Her dad picked her up after her shift at the corner shop on alternate Saturdays. They stopped, as they always did at the bookies on the way back to his and Tracy's house.

'Won't be a minute, sweetheart, just a quick Saturday punt on the gee-gees. You bring me luck you know.' When he came back, he tossed a bag of crisps and a Mars Bar onto her lap. 'Let's not tell Tracy about this,' he said, winking at Amy as he drove off.

Amy didn't know if she wasn't to mention the bookies or the crisps and chocolate. Maybe both.

She heard Kev slam out the front door on Saturday evening, leaving a trail of aftershave lingering for too long in the hallway.

'Don't be too late, darling,' Tracy called uselessly after the door had banged shut. 'Boys,' she said fondly to no one in particular and snuggled down on the sofa with Amy's dad to watch Match of the Day. Amy excused herself after a stultifyingly boring half-hour with them. All three munching on popcorn, her dad roaring his approval when his team scored a goal and groaning loudly when they missed an opportunity.

Amy sat on her bed flicking through the messages on her group chat. All her school mates were out on the town in McDonalds or hanging about the shopping centre. All, apparently, having a great time. Amy sighed. She had not been able to get onto Kev's group chats. She had no idea when he would be coming home, but she had a plan for Sunday morning…

Her dad and Tracy always had a couple of hours of 'alone time' as Tracy coyly put it, on Sunday mornings after breakfast. As soon as they disappeared, Amy hastily changed into the black jeans and the long-length purple sweater she had bought in the charity shop with what little money was left over from her wage after she had put aside her weekly instalment for her mum. She applied the dark pink lipstick, arranged her lips into a pout and made for the stairs. As an afterthought, she turned back and left her glasses on the table, wishing that she had brought the blue eyeshadow with her as well. Never mind, she was determined that Kev would recognise that she was grown up now.

She crept up the stairs and put her ear against Kev's bedroom door to check that he was inside. For a moment there was no sound. Then she heard a muffled giggle. It was a girl. Kev had a girl in his bedroom – she must have been there all night...

Amy froze. Then from her toes to her head, a wave of despair rose up, pouring through every cell in her body. A tsunami of grief. She turned to rush back downstairs but tripped blindly over a pile of trainers and socks discarded outside Kev's bedroom door. She stumbled awkwardly into the door but before she could straighten up and escape, the door was yanked open and she almost fell into the room.

'What the fuck...?' Kev grabbed her wrist and pulled her into his room, shutting the door behind him. He was wearing only boxer shorts and his body odour was strange and musky.

She could see the out-of-focus outline of someone in the bed, sheets pulled up but strands of blonde hair escaping onto the pillow. Fifteen-and-a-half-year-old Sally-Anne Herbertson stuck her head up and glared at Amy.

Kev was in her face. 'If you tell my mum about this, I'll kill you,' he hissed in a loud stage whisper. 'Geddit?'

'Don't worry about her, babe,' said Sally-Anne. 'Four-eyes won't say anything at school either. She knows that would be a big mistake. Look at the state of her! Lipstick and no glasses on. She fancies you. Pathetic!'

Amy fled. Humiliated. How could she have been

so stupid to even think that Kev would like her? She just wanted to die. She wrote a quick note to her dad saying that she had to go home to finish some homework for school. It took her two hours to get across town back home. There were few buses – Sunday service – and she had no money for a taxi.

Amy refused to go to school, claiming stomach pains, sickness and headaches until, on day three, her mum threatened her with a visit to the GP to get a sick note. That was the rule.

Finally, she went back to school but was bombarded with horrible messages on Snapchat from several of the group, taunting her with hideous insinuations or just calling her hurtful names. It was unbearable. She told her dad that she was now working all day on Saturdays at the corner shop, so she couldn't stay over. He accepted her story and, instead, offered to take her out for lunch on their next Sunday at a nearby service station on the southbound M25. He liked the slot machines there.

Amy got a private message on her phone the first Saturday after her humiliating experience with Kev.

'Hi, this is Jim Anderson. We are in the same maths group. I am looking for a study buddy for maths. Interested?'

Amy was astonished and very surprised to hear from Jim Anderson. He was a quiet, studious lad who also wore glasses. She had not noticed his name on the group chats before. He was top of the class in maths and she was struggling with the subject. With GCSEs looming the following year, this could be the answer for her.

'Hi Jim. Yes, I would be interested but you probably know that I am not very good at maths and might hold you back.'

'That's not a problem Amy. I really want to get to know you better.'

They exchanged several private messages over the weekend until Amy began to think that perhaps he really did like her. He asked if he could meet her before school on Monday morning to discuss their plan for working together on their maths homework.

'Where are you off to so early?' her mum asked her on Monday morning. Amy had been so depressed and down recently, hardly leaving her bedroom, but today her daughter seemed to be unusually animated.

Amy blushed. 'Oh, Mum. I'm meeting Jim Anderson from my school at the park this morning. We are going to be study buddies for maths. I think he likes me, Mum.'

'Well just you be careful. You know what boys can be like at that age. All raging hormones.'

'Oh, Mum, Jim is a quiet boy. He's not like that.'

'Hmm…' Amy's mum watched her girl walk down the road, swinging her schoolbag.

On an impulse, she grabbed her car keys and went out the door.

Amy stood under the big oak tree in the middle of the park, a favourite meeting place for the local teenagers. The only other people out so early were a couple walking a lively spaniel puppy in the distance. There was no sign of Jim Anderson, but Amy suddenly became aware of a group of schoolgirls approaching her at a rapid trot. She saw the bright blonde ponytail swinging as the leader of the group drew nearer. It was Sally-Anne Herbertson.

'Hello loser. Who are you waiting for? Not Kev by any chance?'

'No, no,' Amy stammered, suddenly feeling fear as the girls surrounded her. 'I'm meeting Jim Anderson. We're going to work on our maths together.'

'Hear that, girls? This fat pig thinks that anyone, even that swot Jim Anderson would be interested in her. Look at her! Too stupid to recognise a set-up.' With that, Sally-Anne pushed Amy so hard that she lost her balance, her glasses flying off her face as she went down. Her face was pushed into the flattened grass, someone yanked at her hair and someone else kicked her in the back. Through her sobbing screams, she heard her mum's voice yelling,

'Get off her, you cowardly bitches. I know who you are. You'll pay for this.'

Back at home, after her mum had taken her straight to the GP and then on to the police station to report the assault, they sat together on the sofa. Amy was still traumatised.

'Whatever happens, darling, you are not going back to that school. They are vile bullies. I'll look for another job in Norfolk, where I grew up. And though it may take some time, we'll find you a nice school to go to. If your dad wants to see you, he'll have to come and visit you. I am going to look after you and get you some help until you are better. I am so sorry. I just didn't realise what you were going through. You will soon forget all this. I promise you.'

Amy sighed and leaned against her mum. It would never be better.

3. *Lasting Love*

MIRROR, MIRROR

Louise Norton

I see her
as only I can.

She sweeps her silver hair
into a style that knows her well,
includes the clasp lovingly given
when her hair was fair.

I watch.

Pale eyes look back
reflecting a million moments ago.
Eyelids glisten pearly blue;
lipstick of cherry deftly drawn.

He stands, prepares.
I look at him too.
He returns the glance.
I spy from my point of view.

His white hair now few to form
replaces waves of raven that went before;

dimpled face so comfortably worn.
Dark eyes look back.

I detect what you reflect.

She smiles in her turquoise elegance,
oh, so approving of what I disclose.
He, with violet tie, in his pinstriped suit,
happy with what I expose.

I watch them leave,
fade-away
out of my sight.

Closing the door…
keeping fifty years of delight
safe and sound.
Off to their celebration,
holding each other goldenly tight…

LUCKY DIP

Jane MacKinnon

Celia shook her honey-blonde bob in wonderment at the chaos of my kitchen. On the floor, surrounded by scrunched up paper and scraps of corrugated cardboard, lay a disembowelled packing case marked 'Misc'. Its contents covered every horizontal surface.

'Coffee? Do sit down,' I invited.

She scanned the room again and removed a small beechwood box from the seat of a chair. As she placed it on the table, she lifted its clasps, carefully protecting her manicured nails. 'Paints!' she exclaimed. 'How sweet. You never mentioned you painted.' She closed the lid again.

'I haven't touched them for years,' I said, hunting around for two clean mugs.

'Well you should enrol in one of the courses they're holding at the Manor House during Arts Week. There are still vacancies. I know because the tutor is a friend of mine.'

'It would be nice,' I said, 'but I really must get on with unpacking. It's only instant, I'm afraid.'

'Rubbish.' Celia, usually so poised, looked flustered for a moment. 'I didn't mean the coffee.' I bet she did, subconsciously. Celia had a fancy Heston Blumenthal espresso machine; own-brand *Rich & Smooth* had no place on her palate. 'I meant,' she continued hastily, 'that those boxes have been in your garage for at least six months. Another week won't make any difference. No milk, please.'

'Biscuit?'

She shook her head emphatically. 'I know,' she went on, obviously struck by a good idea, 'I'll invite the course tutors round for drinks. Then you can meet Benedict…'

'Lovely,' I lied.

What, I wondered later, does one wear for 'drinks'?

The awful words 'smart casual' came to mind and I mentally rummaged through my wardrobe in search of such garments. I had somewhere, I was sure, a black silky top with a touch of diamante… or sequins? I couldn't remember. It was a long time since I'd socialised with strangers.

Physically rummaging through the boxes marked 'Bedroom' was disheartening. All sorts of unsuitable apparel littered the floor before I found the top I had in mind. It lay crumpled at the bottom of the second-to-last box and was smaller than I recalled. *Oh well, you can't go wrong with black,* I thought.

You can, of course. As soon as I walked into Celia's opulent living room I felt like a carrion crow in the midst of an aviary of birds of paradise. It was not as though I hadn't been told: they were all artists. I hovered by the door, matching the outfits to the craft. Colour-blocked dress in red and blue: stained glass teacher. Bangles and dangling beads: jewellery. And the woman in the, er, rustic skirt must teach home spinning and weaving. Celia beckoned me into the room.

'Susan, take a seat and I'll get you a drink,' she instructed. 'This is John. He's a potter.'

John squirmed round in the sofa and nodded. Bit of a dish, himself, I thought. He had a warm smile and looked comfortable – by build and nature, rather than by seating position. He was wearing a jumper with an abstract floral pattern in deep crimsons and blues, all outlined with a darker hue. Obviously channelling Moorcroft. 'Oviform,' I imagined the descriptive label would say.

'Pleased to meet you,' I said, lowering myself onto the sofa.

Why do people have these long, low sofas? Too late I understood why Celia only ever sat daintily on an *arm* of a sofa, never in one. Once I had sunk into its jaws, I was powerless to move. Like an insect in a Venus flytrap, I felt my body being slowly assimilated into the soft creamy flesh of the upholstery. Then I was given a glass of wine – a 1996 Margaux, explained Celia so nonchalantly that I knew I should be impressed – and all hope of escape was gone.

Celia flitted about the room, glass in one hand, topping-up bottle in the other, having brief but apposite conversations with each of her guests: restoring the stained-glass windows in our mediaeval church; the type of sheep's wool used for her handmade tweed cushion covers; the best sort of wood for a novice carver.

'What do you think of my Lucy Rie?' She alighted like a butterfly on the corner of the coffee table and indicated the large shallow stoneware bowl at the centre.

'Very nice indeed,' said John. 'Early 1960s isn't it?' Celia beamed and floated away happily. 'Dread to think what she paid for it,' he muttered. 'Tens of thousands.'

'For a bowl?' I asked incredulously. 'Can it be worth it?'

'Well,' he said, 'to my mind it would be worth more if there was something in it.'

I rather liked John.

The wine flowed freely but conversation did not. Unable to move forward in our seats we had to shout across the wide coffee table. Most people gave up and, in the ensuing pauses, I could hear – as I'm sure could everyone – the rumblings of my stomach. I became obsessed with the need for food.

I began to fantasise about an unseen team of professional caterers beavering away, about to amaze us all with… with *something*. A sausage roll would do. I sniffed surreptitiously in the direction of the kitchen. I could detect the tang of lime, the pungent clove-y smell of basil, the sweetness of mandarin… but that was the Jo Malone room fragrance. There was not a whiff of anything edible.

Now that I thought about it, I had never seen Celia eat. Her fashionably slim figure, I realised, was the direct result of *not liking food*.

But wait! A plate of olives was placed, with some ceremony, on the coffee table – quite beyond the reach of those trapped in the sofas that flanked it. Two bowls of dips arrived.

'Mmm,' I said encouragingly. 'They look good. What are they?'

I expected some sort of lightweight conversational reply: 'baba ganoush – fell in love with it in the Middle East' perhaps, or 'organic sun-dried tomato houmous, home-made by this super little deli.'

Instead, Celia threw me a look of complete bewilderment. 'Dips,' she said, as if I were mad.

Dips, yes, but sadly, no dippers…

The wine was going to my head. I had to eat something. I spied a bowl of crisps on the far side of the room. The contortions required for exiting the sofa – the *cream* sofa – were simply not possible with a glass of red in my hand. Insulting as it was to such a fine wine, I drained my glass and struggled unsteadily from my well-sprung trap.

On my return I was greeted as something of a hero by my fellow captives, but my triumph was short-lived. The crisps were not up to the job of dipping. Some broke unappetisingly into the dips. Many collapsed halfway between bowl and lips. I was discreetly scraping taramasalata (I now knew what it was) off my left bosom when I felt a tap on my shoulder.

'Susan, I'd like you to meet Benedict. Ben is taking the painting course I was telling you about.'

Standing next to Celia was a tall, strikingly confident man with green – yes, green – hair. 'Celia tells me you paint.' He held out his hand to me.

I mumbled about being terribly out of practice and wondered what the correct etiquette was. Should one boldly engage in the handshake, regardless of one's dip-smeared fingers? Or should one lick them clean first?

In the end, I held both hands out, palms uppermost – a gesture of helplessness and apology. Benedict withdrew his hand.

'We don't do finger painting, I'm afraid,' he said, smirking as he turned away.

I looked miserably at the floor. There was mud on my shoes. Out of the corner of my eye I saw a large vase rolling off the sofa.

John was in front of me, taking my hands – my sticky, unlicked hands – in his. 'These,' he pronounced, 'are the hands of a potter.'

***

John and I make bowls. We sell mainly at craft fairs although some of John's larger pieces have been stocked by Liberty. People buy them solely for their decorative appeal, which annoys him. 'You should never separate the form from the function,' he grumbles, 'and for the past ten thousand years the primary function of a bowl has been to contain food.' He has a specific picture in mind for every bowl he makes: filled to its earthenware brim with a spiced lentil soup… bubbling over with the juices of a steak and ale pie… piled high with fruits like a Dutch still life.

My works are more modest: small bowls, the sort you use for olives or nuts. Or dips.

BAR CODE

Louise Norton

Feelin' you perusing my perimeter,
darkly lookin' in your disco shirt.
I was twirling on my soft bar stool
and you stirred a cherry
in my cocktail heart.

Slide on over to my side (show)
an' I'll pucker my lips
an' rearrange my hair.

Your azure eyes dance to the beat;
makes me blush
feelin' the heat.

Wanna come over and occupy my space?
Wanna come over, wanna come over?
Reachin' out for your embrace…

Playin' so cool in my smouldering dress;
reelin' me in as you crack a smile
My mouth drops open, saying:
'Do you wanna stay for a while?'

Wanna occupy my soul
with a taste of rock 'n' roll?
Passions rising, temperatures soar,
beating hearts race for the door.

Breakin' the bar code.
Crackin' the bar code.

ON STAND-BY IN JULY

Jane MacKinnon

You're at the airport. Might get on a flight.
Unlikely, I think, at this time of night.
In the dark house, I feel your absence loom.
I see bright stand-by lights in every room.
Blue on the microwave. On the fridge, green.
Red on the phone and answering machine.
TVs, printer – I stop counting at eight.
Twelve, says the clock (in blue).
                                    Who flies so late?
Even the laptop sleeps, pulsing soft white.
Out in the garden, neon points of light
indicate the places where glow worms wait
on stand-by like me, hoping for a mate.

The male of the species has wings to fly.

OUT OF THE MIST

Pat Abercromby

Gerda shivered in the cold wind blowing off the North Sea. The pale winter sunshine glinted off the imposing granite buildings, the embedded crystals of quartz, feldspar and mica sparkling a promising welcome. 2007, Aberdeen, the Granite City, pride of the North East of Scotland, her new home, her new future.

Andrius, the surly Lithuanian agent who had recruited her and three other girls four weeks previously, had taken them straight from the airport to the fish processing factory near Peterhead fish market on Harbour Road, to show them where it was.

'Your first shift starts at 7 a.m. tomorrow. Don't be late. There are plenty of other girls looking for work here,' Andrius growled. He pointed towards a dark grey, shabby tenement building that they could just see at the far end of Harbour Road. 'Check in there with the landlady, a Mrs Campbell, she will show you to your rooms. You must give her a week's rent in advance. Don't mess with her or you will be out on the street.' With that, Andrius left them to find their own way and hurried off in his hired car.

Gerda clutched the small suitcase that she had been allowed to take on the budget flight from

Vilnius International Airport. The sharp edges of the cheap leather handle cut into her hand. She was exhausted after the turbulent flight from her homeland. Shrugging off her anxiety, she straightened her back and raised her chin a little, ready to meet whatever challenges lay ahead of her. After all, she thought, her ten years of working in a chemical plant in Kaunus had offered nothing but harsh, unrewarding tasks with nothing to show for it. She was horrified at how the waste products from the factory polluted the atmosphere and the waterways. Moscow's uncaring exploitation and toxic legacy to her country. She had been glad to leave it all behind.

Her bedsit was dark, smelled mouldy and was sparsely furnished with a single bed, a chest of drawers and a sagging armchair, but Gerda did not care, she was determined to make the most of this new opportunity. She slept restlessly that first night, anxious not to be late and was standing outside the factory before 7 a.m.

The minute the doors to the factory opened, the pungent fishy smell flooded her senses and she recoiled, almost gagging. *This is going to take some getting used to,* Gerda thought, breathing through her mouth as she pushed her feet into the icy insides of blue rubber boots, at least two sizes too big for her. *Tomorrow I will wear three pairs of socks,* she decided as her toes began to freeze, even as she stuffed her fair curls into a mesh net held in place with a hard, plastic white cap. She shrugged into the supplied starched white overalls and finally, around her waist, she tied a stiff, heavy blue rubber apron that hung below her knees.

Clutching the thick rubber gloves supplied, Gerda took her place at her station on the endless production lines stretching the whole length of both sides of the cavernous factory. In the middle aisle stood the baskets of North Sea bounty, mostly cod and haddock packed in ice, waiting to be gutted and filleted. The other new recruits, women and girls, many of them from Eastern Europe like her, were waiting for the supervisor to show them the technique of gutting and filleting the fish. The gloves were to protect her hands from frostbite through handling the sharp-edged heavy fish boxes. It was tricky controlling the filleting knife through the gloves and her fingers soon became chafed and sore. Although her English was poor, she picked up the technique quickly and knew that the supervisor was pleased with her. All the filleting stations had their own hosepipe to wash down the filleting slab between batches; the fish scales and slime stuck stubbornly to her apron and gloves, although most of the slippery fish guts and scales flowed over the small concrete platform she was standing on and into the shallow channel below her feet. A noisome stream of fishy detritus.

'Hey, you, what's your name, Gerda? Come with me, the boss wants to see you.' The foreman barked at her in his thick Doric accent. She stopped and looked at him, puzzled. She made out the word 'boss' and 'come with me' wondering anxiously why the boss wanted to see her. Had she done something wrong? She had kept her head down and worked hard for the past week. She desperately needed her wages. Her small float of money was almost gone. Mrs Campbell, her formidable landlady, would be looking for the next week's rent. It was Friday afternoon and the end of another long shift, standing on her feet all day in the smelly, echoing production line. She wondered how long her aching legs and feet would last out before she developed the thick, ropey, varicose veins that her mother suffered from.

She rushed to her locker and quickly peeled off the rubber gloves encrusted with slime and fish scales, undid her thick plastic apron and pulled off the overalls, the white plastic cap and net, slipped her frozen feet out of the unyielding blue rubber boots and into her shoes. Her fair, springy curls, released from their scratchy confines, tumbled around her shoulders. She hurried after the lopsided, retreating figure of the short foreman. The boss was sitting at his desk in the small office overlooking the factory floor. Gerda had often seen his face at the window. Sometimes he stood looking out at them for ages.

'Shut the door behind you, Billy.'

The foreman nodded at his boss and left.

'Well lass,' he continued, coming out from behind his desk and perching on the end of it. His swinging leg, clad in shiny, dark blue material, was inches from Gerda. She could smell the staleness of him, overlaid with alcohol. 'You're a good worker, I've been watching you. I've got your wage packet here.' He held out the small brown envelope with her money.

Gerda reached out her hand to take the envelope, murmuring, 'Thank you.' But with snake-like speed, he grabbed her hand and pushed it into his crotch. She gasped and tried to pull away from him. 'Ne! Ne!'

He used his steely strength to push her against the wall and tried to force his foul-tasting tongue between her teeth, one hand painfully dragging her hair to pin her head in place. She was jammed against his grinding hips, her lower body trapped. His free hand ripped and plunged at her breast.

'C'mon, I know you Litho girls like a bit of extra action. You want your pay packet? Then play the game.' His coarse breathy voice rasped thickly in her ear.

The bile of fear and rage filled her throat. Gerda struggled with manic energy to free herself. She managed to pull away far enough to bring her knee up sharply, connecting with his groin.

'Effing bitch!' he snarled, his fist smashing into her cheek. 'You're fired! Eff off out of here and don't let me see your ugly face again!' He threw her wage packet on the floor and turned his back on her, swigging deeply from a bottle of Scotch that he yanked out of the desk drawer.

Gasping for breath, Gerda grabbed her money and fled through the door. By now, the others had left and the big factory hall was deserted. The floor was wet with melting ice and fish scales. At the far end, a cleaner was noisily hosing down the benches, singing tunelessly at the top of his voice. His back was turned and he could not have seen or heard her leave. Her erratic heartbeat thudded, the pain from the punch had left her reeling. She could feel her eye swelling and closing. The shocked tears blinded her further as she stumbled along the road that ran alongside the harbour.

It was dark now and a thick coastal mist, the haar, was rolling in off the North Sea, encasing Gerda in oppressive misery. What was she to do now? She had no job and no prospects of getting another one easily.

Andrius, the Lithuanian agent had arranged all the work visas and got her the job at the fish factory. Her English was not good enough to apply for jobs herself... On and on her thoughts ran and her despair deepened. Maybe she should report her boss to the police, but would they believe her? Where was the police station? They might deport her if she had no work. *Oh God, what should I do?* she agonised.

She didn't see the grill set into the edge of the pavement. The water from another harbour-side fish processing factory had been brushed out through the open doors down through the grill, eventually adding its fishy effluent to the churning sea water. Still blinded by tears and with her eye almost completely closed from the swelling of the brutal punch, her foot caught in the dip of the grill and she fell headlong. Her hands splayed out and the treacherous wind grabbed her wage packet, whistling it out of her grasp, bouncing and rolling away until it disappeared into the thickness of the haar. Gerda howled in piercing distress. Dragging herself into a sitting position on the cold, damp pavement, she clasped her knees, bowed her head and rocked back and forth, back and forth...

***

That was how he found her. He had just dropped off a couple of oil rig engineers at the heliport as they prepared to return to their off-shore rig for another three week stretch. He was driving slowly back home along Harbour Road and had cracked open the passenger windows to air out the cab. Those riggers hadn't showered. He first heard the unearthly keening but couldn't tell at first if it was a human voice or a mortally wounded animal. It sent shivers down his spine. Peering through the fog, he saw the huddled shape on the pavement. Carefully, he stepped out of his taxi and approached the shape, realising as he grew closer, that this was a fair-haired woman, her face buried in her arms, sobbing and rocking.

'Oh lassie, fit's wrong? Are you hurt?' He bent down and touched her arm gently. Her head flew up, arms flailing wildly, pushing his hand away.

'Ne! Ne! Don't touch me!' She screamed at him in Lithuanian and of course he could not understand her words, but fully got the message. He was horrified to see one side of her face swollen and distorted, her eye completely closed. He saw the scraped and bloodied hands and the dark patches of blood seeping through the knees of her trousers.

He crouched down beside her. 'Lass, lass, I won't hurt you. Let me help you. You need to get to a hospital.' He kept his tone as even and gentle as possible. This girl was in deep shock. Whoever had done this to her, probably a man, he guessed, had destroyed her trust. He needed her to trust him. He looked straight into her damaged face, 'I promise you, I won't harm you,' he repeated, gently keeping eye contact with her. She stared at him for a few moments before trying to scrabble to her feet. He thought she might try to flee from him, but she stood swaying, allowing him to steady her. At that moment, as he felt her body relax against him, he knew that she would let him help her.

They sat for three hours in the A&E in Aberdeen Royal Infirmary before Gerda was seen. He stayed with her, feeling oddly protective. In the harsh light of the waiting room, he could see that she was probably in her late twenties and possibly quite pretty, but her poor face was so swollen, it was hard to tell. The purple lake of livid bruising was spreading by the minute.

At first, she didn't speak and he could see that she was shaking, still in shock and pain. He brought them both a cup of tea. After a while the warmth of the drink seemed to ease her and she stopped trembling. Gerda knew a few words of English and haltingly, managed to tell him what had happened to her. He stayed calm, quietly encouraging her to tell her story. Later. Later he would avenge her.

Gerda's eyes drooped and her head rested lightly on Graham's shoulder. He felt pleased, she must be feeling more at ease with him. It was a while since a woman had shown any warmth towards him, he realised. His nearly ex-wife was a nightmare, demanding more and more money from him as the date for their divorce and the final settlement drew near. He just needed it all to be over and done with. His stomach was playing up again. It was probably stress, his GP had told him.

'Miss?' The young doctor came into the cubicle. Gerda opened her eyes and looked panicky again.

'She doesn't speak much English,' Graham explained, smiling reassuringly at Gerda.

'Are you her husband?' enquired the doctor.

'No, no,' his face flushed, 'I'm Graham, I'm just a friend.'

'Okay, but can you tell her I want to examine her face and check out her other injuries?'

Gerda winced as the medic felt round her damaged cheek and eye socket. Instinctively, Graham placed his hand on her shoulder as the doctor completed his examination. Her hands and knees were badly scraped but didn't require any stitches.

'I am sending you for an X-ray to make sure that the cheek bone and eye socket are not fractured. You'll have to report this assault to the police.'

'Aye,' Graham replied for her, 'we will, don't you worry.'

'We have a Polaroid camera in the department, I will give you a photograph of her injuries for future evidence if you want,' the young doctor added kindly, keen to help.

Graham explained to Gerda what the doctor had said, and she nodded, beyond caring. Every part of her body was aching and painful.

Graham went with her to the X-ray Department and helped her negotiate the radiologist's instructions. They went back to the A&E doctor who confirmed that there was no fracture, just soft tissue damage. After another wait at the pharmacy to collect painkillers and anti-inflammatory tablets, they found themselves standing, suddenly awkwardly, outside the hospital.

'Do you want to go to the police station now and report the assault?' Graham spoke slowly, using simple hand gestures so that she would understand him.

She shivered and shook her head vigorously. 'Home. Go tomorrow.' It was late. He could see that she was exhausted. Graham nodded and gently holding her arm, led her to his taxi.

She wrote down her address for him and he drove her home. He took her right up to her door and waited, unsure, while she opened the door. She turned to him.

'Please, come in.'

Graham had just had time to take in the shabbiness of the bare little bedsit when there was a loud hammering at the door. He opened the door to be confronted by a furious Mrs Campbell, Gerda's landlady.

'No men are allowed in these rooms. You can pack your bags and get out.' She pushed past Graham and angrily confronted Gerda who was sitting on the edge of her bed, her bandaged hands resting on her ripped and blood-stained trousers. 'Good grief! What's happened to you?'

Graham quickly explained what had happened and that Gerda would not be able to work until she had recovered from her injuries.

'Well, she can stay here if she can pay the rent but if she can't, she will have to leave. I'm not running a charity.'

'Let her sleep here tonight and tomorrow I will come back for her. My sister has a spare room. We'll look after her.' Graham fished around in his pocket and handed Mrs Campbell two crumpled ten-pound notes.

Mrs Campbell sniffed and pushed the money into a pocket in her apron. 'Make sure she's gone by ten o'clock, I need to get this room cleaned before I can rent it out again.'

Gently, Graham explained as clearly as he could to Gerda, that tomorrow he would come back for her and take her to the police station to report the assault and then take her to his sister's house where she could stay for as long as she needed.

She understood most of what he told her, but

looking into his kind, concerned face, she knew that she could trust this man and that she would let him help her. Suddenly she was beyond thinking, the effects of the shock and the strong painkillers swept away all awareness and she lay down on her back and slept. Graham covered her carefully with a blanket and left.

***

It had been a challenging year for Graham. His difficult ex-wife had brought two children with learning difficulties into the marriage. He had done his best to be a good stepfather for them. The girl had a similar temperament to her mother and was extremely oppositional, but the wee boy adored Graham and followed him around all the time, asking questions which Graham would answer patiently, even although the boy never seemed to fully grasp the answers. As part of the divorce settlement, Graham had agreed to let her stay in the marital home with her kids, hoping that she would agree to look after his beloved black Labrador, Maisie. He was not allowed to have a pet in his first-floor apartment. At first, his ex let him come to the house every day to collect Maisie and take her for a walk, but she kept complaining that Maisie's hair was getting everywhere and it was too much for her to cope with now that she had to run the house by herself. Graham had done most of the chores when he lived with her.

'That bloody dog is going to have to go. I need a new carpet now. She's ruined the hall one with her scraping and scratching,' she whinged, aiming a swipe at Maisie who slunk low on her belly behind Graham.

'Please, just give me a bit more time. My pal Keith

is renovating his house near Hazelhead Park and he'll take the dog. He's got a big garden and it backs onto open fields. It will be perfect for Maisie and I can still walk her. Please, Jean, it won't be for much longer.'

But, within the week, Jean secretly gave Maisie away to a farmer somewhere in the Borders and refused to tell Graham where she was. Devastated and angry, he could have killed his vicious ex-wife but, as always, he stepped away, mindful that the wee boy was watching him with frightened eyes.

***

After living with Graham's sister for a few weeks while she recovered from the physical signs of her assault, Gerda moved in with Graham. They were dating by now and had grown close despite the language barrier. Graham was consumed with helping Gerda bring her boss to justice and it distracted him from the gnawing pain of losing his dog. As Gerda's English was so limited, Graham attended all the meetings she had to have with the prosecuting barrister and supported her through the harrowing ordeal of giving evidence against her boss in Court.

It turned out that he had assaulted several of the other Eastern European factory girls as well, and they came forward to complain when Gerda's story became public. He was given a five-year prison sentence. Not nearly long enough, his victims thought. He was released three years into his sentence for 'good behaviour' but was arrested again a year later. This time for people-trafficking. One of the key witnesses in the case was a local taxi driver who had made it his business to follow the activities of the perpetrator after he was released from prison. Some may have called it stalking, but Graham finally got his revenge against the person who had so traumatised his lovely partner. They both felt that justice had at last been done and for Gerda, it gave her some closure.

Graham helped Gerda find a job as a cleaner in one of the hotels near Dyce Airport. The hotel was so clean and warm! She had to work hard and fast, cleaning twelve bedrooms in an eight-hour shift, but it was so much better than the fish processing factory.

In the evenings, in his small, one-bedroomed flat, they watched movies together to help Gerda improve her English. Graham had managed to get his head round a few Lithuanian words so that he could at least exchange the basic pleasantries with her mother on their planned visit to Lithuania the following month. He had just received his passport. His first. He had never been abroad before.

Gerda laughed at his accent, but it was mutual: Graham laughed every time his sister came to visit them.

'Come awa in,' Gerda would say, perfectly reproducing the broad Aberdonian dialect.

4. Love Lost

THE WINDMILL

Pat Abercromby

Vera Jones, recently widowed, from Porthcawl, South Wales, was enjoying a seven-day Caribbean cruise around the Paradise Islands. This was her first holiday since her late husband Thomas had to take early retirement from his job at Barry Docks due to an industrial accident. The cruise was paid for with part of Thomas's compensation money. It had taken seven years for his case to come to court and be agreed. The ship, Cunard's *Queen Elizabeth* had just docked at St John's Port, Antigua, six days into the cruise and the penultimate stop before sailing on to Barbados, where Vera would disembark for the flight home.

Vera had made friends on board with another Saga singleton, Rita, also widowed, from Harrogate in Yorkshire. Vera and Rita were strolling along the endless stretch of the beach at Dickenson Bay a short walk from the ship.

Vera was feeling a tad overheated in her pink cotton top with the three-quarter length sleeves. In truth, the top was also a bit tight over her tummy. She had piled on a few pounds since Thomas… The full-length pink white and green floral-patterned summer trousers had been chosen for her by Thomas, the day they had excitedly booked the cruise. Vera was not too sure about the garish trousers, not quite her taste, but Thomas had loved them and told her she looked like a 'real posh tourist'. She glanced enviously at Rita, short and skinny, wearing a sleeveless candy-striped blue sundress. She looked cool and comfortable in her big sunglasses and wide-brimmed sun hat. *Mind you,* Vera thought, *those upper arms of Rita's are still flapping like bats' wings and those varicose veins on the backs of her legs look like a map of the London Underground.* Still, who would bother looking at them, two old ladies on a cruise? *I wish Thomas was here, he would have loved all this,* she thought as they stopped to gaze at the cobalt blue sea, calm as a millpond, the white, tropical sand warming the soles of their feet through their thin-soled summer sandals. Vera clutched a child's colourful windmill a bit tighter.

'Can you take a picture for me please, Rita cariad? Make sure you include the windmill.'

Vera posed for her picture, the windmill prominently framed as it turned weakly in the gentle tropical breeze.

'Ee that does look lovely if I say so meself. But why the windmill, Vera luv?' Rita was pleased, most of her photographic efforts either had part, if not all, of the subjects' heads missing.

'Well, look you,' explained Vera, 'Thomas used it in the garden to scare off the birds from the cabbages. He loved being in the garden. One minute there he was, hoein' between the weeds. Next minute, dead as a dodo.'

Vera paused. 'At least he didn't suffer.' Her voice cracked. 'He had a good send-off mind. The

Porthcawl male voice choir sang two choruses of "Men of Harlech". Not a dry eye in the house. Thomas had booked this cruise months in advance. Non-refundable. He would have hated to waste the money. So here I am. I brought the windmill instead of Thomas.'

'Time for cocktails, Vera luv.' Rita linked her arm through Vera's plump one, giving it a little sympathetic squeeze.

They turned and walked slowly back toward the massive cruise ship glinting white and inviting in the setting sun. The windmill twirled cheerfully in the warm tropical breeze.

STUFFED HEART

Jane MacKinnon

Start with a heart that is tender and sweet
for a heart grows tougher with every beat.
Salt onions with tears; leave thyme in between;
add sage for the person you could have been
had you coddled with warmth, not burnt with fire,
and not outweighed love with rough-cut desire.
An over-filled heart, even trussed, will burst.
When you stuff the next heart, learn from the first.

PERFUME

Sarah-Jane Reeve

Opening the door
to a perfume store
on a rainy afternoon,
caught in a crowd
I was suddenly kissed
by your scent
of rosemary,
musk
and moss.

Then the past rushed up to greet me,
and memories put their arms around me
as I stood there.
Alone.

THERE YOU ARE

Louise Norton

There you are, tucked up in my heart.
My mind captures all of you.

Joy dances around your smile,
timeless and perfect.

There you are soaring through the sky,
wild and wondrous you shine so bright.

There you go, back into my heart,
fitting snugly forever.

A tribute to the dancer, Christopher Kindo.

Christopher Kindo and Louise Norton in 'Footprints'
choreographed by Val Delys Steyn for Jazzart.
Cape Town, S.A. 1981

Lyrics from the E.P.
by Norton and Stutterheim
Photographer: Beni Stillborg

GRIEF, MY DARK COMPANION

Jane MacKinnon

When we became acquainted, so many years ago,
you never left my side. Where I went, you would go,
forcing me to see all things through your unhappy eyes.
You dulled the brightest sun; you blacked the
    bluest skies.

Tell me, dark companion, how long must bleakness last?
Is my future doomed to be as painful as my past?
Time, I always understood, will mend a damaged heart
so, though we cling together, it's time for us to part.

But one of us – I can't say which – will not let go.
You watch me from the crowd, seeing I feel alone,
at a party, in the shops, going to a show.
'Remember me?' you ask. 'Are you still on your own?'
And I, while dearly wishing we had never met,
greet you as a friend and say, 'How can I forget?

FINDING LILY

Pat Abercromby

'I want my mum,' Lily wailed. She clutched the
nurse's fingers tightly, her hands slick with sweat,
nails digging in, blue eyes wide with terror as another
tearing contraction ripped through her skinny,
adolescent body.

'I want to go home!'

'It won't be long now. You are a very brave girl.
Baby is nearly here. One more big push…'

Afterwards, the midwife struggled to get the image
out of her head: the girl, no more than a child herself,
terrified, asking for her mother – and alone. No
sixteen-year-old girl should have to endure giving
birth without the reassuring support of her mother, or
at least a relative. Where were they?

'What are you going to call your baby girl?' she
asked the weeping girl gently as she carefully stitched
up the ragged tear that the baby's difficult exit had left
in the tender flesh.

'I… I don't know.' She looked doubtfully at the
sleeping newborn swaddled in the crib at her bedside.
'What's your name?' The midwife was the only person
who had spoken kindly to her since she was admitted
to the labour ward many hours before. The stark,

disinfectant odour in the ward imprinted on her memory forever.

'Susan, but everyone calls me Sue.'

'Can I call her Sue, after you?'

Unexpected tears brimmed. The midwife swallowed hard before she looked up at the young girl. 'I would be honoured,' she said.

They allowed her to bottle feed the baby herself for the three days before she was discharged. They had given her something to stop her milk coming. The baby's deep blue, opaque eyes were locked onto her face as she fed, as if she were committing every detail to memory.

'Your dad is here to take you home. Give baby to me please.' As the girl instinctively tightened her grip on the sleeping infant, the nurse, in a gentler tone said, 'We will look after baby for you, don't worry.'

She had been praying that someone in her family would come to the hospital to claim her and her baby, take them both home…

Her dad was waiting for her in the hall outside the ward. 'Your mum's not too well,' he said. 'We have a long drive ahead of us, Lily. Let's get going.'

***

'You are a very special little girl, Penny. Mummy and Daddy chose you to be our baby. We adopted you.' Mummy always hugged her when she repeated this. But only at bedtime. Mummy didn't hug during the day. 'Adopted' must mean that she deserved the hug?

If Daddy tucked her in, he would say, 'We love you, sweetheart,' and kiss her forehead.

'What does "adopted" mean?' She was five.

'Penny, it means that we chose you to be our own very special baby. I have always told you this.' Her mother smiled at her. No hug, it was only the afternoon.

'Josie Morgan said you're not my real mummy. She said my real mummy didn't want me and gave me away.'

Josie: harbinger of bad tidings, Penny's year one classmate and nemesis. She who announced triumphantly that Santa Claus wasn't real. Six of the children in the class cried, including Penny. Mummy said that Santa Claus *was* real and not to listen to Josie's nonsense. So, it was several days before she dared tell her mother what Josie had said.

'Penny, sweetheart, I *am* your mother, but you were born to another lady who was not able to take care of you. She called you Sue, but we wanted you to be called Penny. You can't remember, you were just a tiny baby, only three weeks old. Daddy and I chose you to be *our* baby. You are a very special and very lucky little girl. We love you so much.' Mummy looked as if she were going to cry. Her eyes were shiny, her lips were pressed hard together, her cheeks flaring red.

'But,' said Penny, looking up at her mother, 'why did my real mummy not want me? Was I a bad baby? Will you ever give me away, too, Mummy?' The strange, aching, fluttering feeling in her tummy, had ramped up a notch since Josie Morgan's pronouncement.

'Of course not, Penny! Never say that again! You were not a bad baby. We are so proud of you. You are a wonderful child. Come and sit beside me for a minute.' Her mother patted the space beside her on the sofa and Penny crept into her mother's embrace. The constant, deep, empty feeling in her insides did not go away. *If I am not a bad baby and so special, why did my real mummy not want me?* But her mother had said not to mention it again, so she didn't.

Her baby brother, William, arrived soon after. Her mum and dad had prepared her for his coming and she was excited to learn that he was adopted too and was also very special. She was glad that William's real mother was a lady who also gave her baby away. She was no longer the only child in her family who did not *really* belong to her parents. Mummy and Daddy loved her, they always said so and now they loved her new brother, William. *So, parents can love more than one child? I must try to be a good girl, so they keep on loving me. Why could my real mummy not love me too?*

Once she knew that she had a real mummy, she could not stop thinking about her. In Penny's dreams, she was a luminous being with long, shiny, strawberry blonde hair who would gather her little girl into her arms and sing her to sleep cradled in her soft embrace. Often, when she woke in the morning, the empty feeling would wash over her again. Grumpily, she would pull on the clothes that her mother had left folded neatly on the bedside chair, often kicking one sock under the bed. It made her mum cross, every time. She did not mean to upset her mother, it might be risky to lose her approval, but she just couldn't stop the big, nameless, angry feeling that was growing inside her.

'Penny, for goodness' sake stop losing your sock. Look under the bed. It must be there. I think you do this deliberately, just to annoy me. Hurry. You will be late for school and lose one of your silver stars. You want to be pupil of the week, don't you?'

It would be years before Penny had any understanding of why her mum was so exasperated (and hurt) by her apparent oppositional attitude; that she couldn't perceive why, when they did everything they could to give the child a good, comfortable life, the five-year-old Penny was acting out almost every day. She must have wondered what she was doing wrong, why the child never showed any real affection towards her, why she seemed to prefer her dad's company. At the time, William must have seemed an easier child.

Penny always got top marks in her class at school: an easy and natural way for her to win the approval of her parents. But she was plump and not much good at sports or gym and short sight forced her to wear ugly, round-rimmed glasses. She was a loner and didn't fit in with the popular girls who clustered around in giggling groups at playtime, or with the sporty ones who ran around playing rounders at lunchtime. She passed her 11 Plus easily to gain a place in a girls-only grammar school. Her parents always praised and encouraged her academic achievements but never pressured her to go on to university. They had both gone straight out to work after leaving school and had no expectations beyond that for their two children. Unlike her brother William, who was casual about school, Penny was driven to prove herself and was determined to continue her education.

Her parents had raised her comfortably and well in their neat, suburban, semi-detached house in the outskirts of Manchester. Her mother stayed at home until her father's redundancy forced her to take a part-time job when Penny was fourteen. The non-negotiable standards that Penny and William had been brought up with remained: clean underwear and socks every day, laundered and ironed school blouses and shirts, good table manners, being polite and consideration for others. And, no questions asked about difficult issues. There were many, but Penny knew better than to give voice to the confusion and rage that often boiled over into frustrated yelling at her mother. It was always at her mother.

'My own mother didn't want me, and you don't want me either! You just don't get me. I'm not like you!' She would slam out of the kitchen, retreat to her bedroom enraged and upset. Unable to understand the anger that was making her head hurt and causing her stomach muscles to cramp. She could not wait to get away from the stultifying lack of communication and emotional connection with her mother. It was guilt. She knew her parents loved her, were good and kind to her, but she felt like an interloper in their lives. An alien, no family history to share with them. No sense of self. Who was she?

Freedom came at last to create an identity away from her parents' boundaries. Manchester University life fed into all of Penny's personality needs. She loved the independence of living away from home. Most of the students on her Computer Technology course were like her, focused and hard-working, not missing lectures and fooling around like some of her new friends in the big four-bedroomed Victorian house they shared. She took up jogging, obsessively dragging herself out of the warmth of bed every morning to grind out a 5k run around the perimeter streets of the campus. Within months she was slim and strong, and her self-confidence improved – although she was wary of forming any romantic relationships with the undergraduates. Her fear of abandonment simmering away subliminally. She graduated with a first and easily found a job in a computer company in Nottingham.

Penny's relationship with her mother was still challenging, although leaving home took some of the heat out of her frustration with her mother's inability to address any difficult situations. Including her father's terminal illness. Not up for discussion. It would have been hard even if they had wanted to, as her dad was always there. Her beloved father died in 1990 without any awareness of Penny's still unacknowledged but growing desire to find her birth mother.

William, her adopted brother, had married and he and his new wife moved back to live near their widowed mother in Manchester. Penny felt easier, less guilty, about accepting another job in a large IT company in Surrey. Her relationship with Alastair who worked in the same company, burned slowly into life. His unwavering determination to win her confidence and trust eventually led to a marriage proposal. Ignoring her ever-present insecurity about lasting loyalty, Penny accepted.

Her mum approved of her boyfriend. Here at last, was Penny fulfilling a normal family tradition, and for once, the two women bonded over the wedding arrangements.

***

Penny was nearly forty before she started looking for

her birth mother. What had stopped her searching for her before then? Guilt? She always knew she was adopted. Special. Chosen. Loved. Why then had she always felt so empty – so angry? Only when she gave birth to her first child did she understand fully the fiercely protective, primitive, unbreakable bond between mother and baby. They were as one, body and soul, conjoined at birth by DNA and memory. If her birth mother had felt this too, how could she have abandoned her baby? She had to find her…

Her need to find her birth mother morphed slowly from a secret, long unacknowledged need, steeped in feelings of disloyalty, to a burning obsession. In 1999, with the rules on searches by adopted children relaxed, she applied for her birth records. Her birth records disclosed the names and ages of her birth mother and father. John and Lily were sixteen and eighteen years old when she was born…

It took her two years of agonising steps, stopping at every stage. Reading the reason for her adoption – her birth mother's own mother was dying of cancer – hit her hard, a cruel stomach punch impossible to reconcile. She was riddled with feelings of intense disloyalty to her adopted mother, all-consuming guilt for continuing to pursue her quest, self-denial of her motives. Specialist counselling sessions helped, and she finally added her name to the Adoption Contact Register. No match.

Devastated, but with her desire to find her birth mother undiminished, Penny continued her search, promising herself that this was an academic exercise only, convincing herself that she would never take this search too far. Would never expose herself at any cost to possible further rejection and hurt. She continued to search for five years, always pursuing new online possibilities, but never getting any closer to finding her birth mother. Then, in 2004, a huge opportunity opened up: online access to Birth, Marriage and Deaths information became available via the General Register Office whose records date back to 1837. Feverishly, Penny applied and paid for birth and marriage certificates for her mother, Lily, and her father, John. Astonishingly, she discovered that her parents had married when they were just in their twenties. But where were they now? Why had they not found a way to keep her with them? She added her name to the NORCAP register (National Organisation for Counselling Adoptees and Parents UK) in March 2004. No matches found there either.

Four months later, almost five years since she first registered with them, she received a letter from the General Register Office to say that a match had been made on the Adoption Contact Register. Penny went into a rapid meltdown. Could this really be happening? Was she close to finding her birth mother? Unable to acknowledge to herself how important the search had become, she told herself that she would not want to take it any further. It would just be a photo exchange, wouldn't it? The photo took agonising, endless attempts to get the 'right' one. Suddenly, she was a child again, seeking approval and acceptance.

Penny knew from her earlier research that, at that time, NORCAP offered an intermediary service to help adoptees and their birth relatives who had made contact. Sick with nerves and anticipation, she sent an introductory letter and photographs to the person who had submitted the matching details via

NORCAP. Four days later she was contacted by a NORCAP intermediary called Jane, a wonderful, understanding lady who told Penny that the contact was actually her cousin who had the same surname – Wilson – as her birth parents and that this cousin Mary had received the letter that Penny had agonised over. She wanted to start corresponding.

With shaking hands, Penny composed the first email to her cousin, a possible link to her birth mother. By return, she received an ecstatic reply from Mary, who explained that Penny's parents had emigrated to New Zealand shortly after they married, and that Penny had a brother. Penny was overwhelmed to learn that it was Lily, her birth mother, who had initiated Mary's help in finding her lost child. She'd tried unsuccessfully for many years – and at this stage neither her husband nor her son knew that she was searching for Penny. She must have been tortured with the prospect of being rejected by Penny. Similarly, Penny did not tell her own three young children that she was searching for her birth mother in case they blabbed this to their grandmother. Penny could not bear to tell her adopted mother: it would feel like a huge betrayal.

Mary wrote again. 'Penny, Lily and John know now that we have made contact with you and are thrilled beyond words. Lily wants to know if she can email you but understands if you are not ready.'

Sick with nerves, Penny replied to say that she was ready to hear from her birth mother. She had so many questions, needed so many answers. There were three more days of obsessively checking her emails before the longed-for message arrived in her inbox. Lily's first letter was tentative, filling Penny in about all the family members she was suddenly connected to, not expressing too many emotions or giving any real explanation about why she gave Penny up for adoption. More emails and photographs were exchanged, and the one-dimensional conceptual family became two dimensional through eagerly searched for shared expressions and likenesses. Gradually the desire to learn more, to see them in real life, overtook Penny's uncertainty. It was finally blown away when her brother wrote to her a few days later. He was upset that he grew up not knowing that he had a big sister, but so delighted to have been told now; that he couldn't wait to meet her and her family and introduce his own children to their new-found cousins. For Penny, it was beyond surreal to become, so suddenly, part of this large extended family who, just a few weeks ago, were totally unknown to her.

**

She stood alone at the Heathrow International Arrivals gate for the Air New Zealand flight from Auckland, feeling like a child again. Anxious. Nervous. What would they think of her, her new family? Was she wearing the right outfit for this first encounter? Her friend had to come shopping with her to help her choose clothes for this visit. She had been incapable of deciding what was appropriate. She had finally decided on a casual look of a white shirt tucked into dark blue linen trousers which showed off her still-trim figure. Her hair, fashionably cropped short at the back with longer sides, framed her face, which she knew from photographs, closely resembled her mother's sister's features. She watched with a fast-beating heart as weary passengers appeared, pushing laden luggage trolleys. Watched their faces lighting up.

Recognition. Saw tears of joy and bear hugs as their relatives rushed forward to greet them. Such a long journey to be reunited with loved ones. *How will it be for us?* she wondered, realising that she was holding her breath. *Breathe. Will I recognise them?* She had an idea what they looked like from photographs. She saw them. Her birth parents. John, balding, sturdy, middle-aged. Lily, no longer the fantasy mother of her childhood with long, strawberry blonde locks. Short, fair, permed hair; face weathered and crinkled around the eyes from exposure to the windy climate of Wellington. They saw her. Penny raised her hand in acknowledgement. For a long moment, they stared at one another, all incapable of movement

'Penny?'

She saw her mother mouth her name. Penny couldn't move.

John grabbed his wife's hand and guided her and the heavy luggage trolley over to Penny.

'Hello kiddo,' he said.

Lily gazed at her daughter, lost for forty-four years – and, unable to hold back any longer – she pulled Penny into an embrace. Penny stiffened in her arms for a moment before the deep well of unknowing in her soul spilled over and she knew at last who she was meant to be. John held back for a few moments before he too came close and put a strong arm around his wife and his daughter. The circle at last complete.

Penny met up with them a few times during their short visit. They stayed with Lily's sister and her husband in East Sussex and Penny visited them there. At last she heard her parents' story.

***

Lily and John were childhood sweethearts. They lived in the same road in Cardiff and had met on the school bus. John's mum had died years before, and his dad was raising him as best he could. Lily fell pregnant when she was still fifteen, and her parents, appalled and ashamed, sent her away to some people they knew in Wrexham, over 150 miles from her home. John, two years older, was forbidden to see her. She was under the age of consent and he could have been charged with, at worst, statutory rape.

The family she stayed with were kind enough, but she was expected to do most of the household chores and to look after the two young children whilst the parents were out at work. She only ever had one visitor from home. John's father, surprisingly, came once or twice and brought her a box of chocolates: Milk Tray, she loved them. Lily, at fifteen and a child of the more austere and less enlightened post-war years was powerless to make choices for herself about her baby's future. She simply had to do what she was told and had to let her baby be taken away from her. In a particularly cruel part of the adoption process back then, she personally had to hand her baby over to the adoption agency after signing paperwork relinquishing any further contact. This was three weeks after being discharged from the hospital and after three weeks of being separated from her baby. Unconscionable.

When she returned home, Lily did not go back to school; instead she found herself as carer for a mum who was dying of cancer. Her career-minded older sister was due to marry and was unwilling to take on Lily's baby. Clearly their dying mother could not help. Many years later, her father confessed that he had wanted to help Lily keep her baby, but without support from the women in his family, he felt helpless.

Lily and John got together again soon after she came home. Neither of them spoke much about the adoption of their baby although John was fully aware that Lily had never fully recovered from her loss and quietly marked each anniversary of the birth. John, naturally reticent, felt it would be easier on Lily if they did not talk about their loss. Lily did the same to protect him from her pain.

*****

The first visit from her brother was an emotional one: both their families were bonding as children of blood do. Penny decided it was time to tell her mother that she had found and met her birth parents and her sibling.

'I always knew you would find her one day,' her mother said. Penny was stricken. Why had her mum never talked to her about this?

'I am glad your dad never knew. He loved you so much.'

'Mum, I am sorry about this, but we are all going to New Zealand to visit John and Lily and my brother's family next month. But I need you to know that nobody could ever take your place. You and Dad are my parents, nothing will ever change that.'

Penny hugged her mother who patted her back. 'Thank you, I am pleased to hear that, and so would Dad have been. We were both very proud of you and the woman you have become. I do love you, you know Penny, I just didn't say it often enough,' she added, as an afterthought.

Penny wished she had said it too.

***

The visit to New Zealand was successful (but oh, how far away) but Penny was struggling with ambivalent feelings about her developing relationship with her new family and her deepening sense of loyalty towards her adopted mother, tempered with anger that they had never communicated properly. She made an appointment with a PAC (Parent Advisory Committee) counsellor, a service for those affected by adoption, which she found very helpful and was sure would help her build bridges with her adoptive mother.

But a month later, her mother had a heart attack and died. Forever lost: the opportunity to reach out to her mother; to try to atone for the irritation and frustration that had marred most of their relationship. Now that the counsellor had helped her understand the unbreakable physical and psychological link a birth mother has with her baby, she was beginning to grasp the difficulties her mother might have experienced in trying to bond with her. Understanding, too, that her mother's own rigid upbringing with emotionally unavailable parents, left her incapable of addressing any real and difficult 'feelings' with her adopted children.

Left in a confusing and devastating whirlwind of guilt and remorse, Penny once again found great comfort in two further sessions with her PAC counsellor; even more from a wonderful, wise, insightful letter from her birth father John, reassuring her that all her feelings and love for the mother and father who raised her could never, nor should they ever, be replaced by her relationship with her newly found birth family. He said in conclusion that he hoped she could find room in her heart to take her place in this family. Not in competition with, or detracting from, the family that raised and nurtured her, but alongside, as a new addition in her life.

**

Fifteen years on, Penny's relationship with her birth family has slowly deepened despite the vast distance between their families that restricts their visits to once a year. In their own ways, they are all still grieving for the lost years, a void that can never be filled completely. However, as she grows closer to her birth family year by year, she has come to realise that, had she not been adopted, none of them would ever have experienced the intense joy and wonder of finding one another. Closing the circle. Complete.

Her children, too, have discovered their roots, their history, and bask in the comfort of the unconditional love and strong bond with their grandparents and their extended family. Belonging.

**

Shortly after Penny made contact with her birth family, her adopted brother also searched for and found his birth parents. Sadly, his story did not end well. Not all stories do.

Ref: The Primal Wound, Understanding The Adopted Child *by Nancy Newton Verrier*

A TRIP TOO FAR

Moyra Zaman

Curly-haired
young Hippy
out of time.

A bustling brain,
creative
to a fault.

Screwing his mind
in drug-filled alleys,
dog-filled, dog-end days.

His 'summer holiday'
– the double-decker dream –
long gone.

Grim November
lurked in corners;
the earth complied

and life withdrew to a dead-end
in smiling tear drops

…to Sting 'In fields of gold'.

ASHES TO ASHES

Jane MacKinnon

It's a rare sight now, the half-filled ashtray.
Or is it half-empty? No-one can know –
all signs of the vice are hidden away.

You used to smoke Gauloise, two packs a day:
inhaling, so deep; exhaling, so slow.
It's a rare sight now, the half-filled ashtray.

You said it kept the mosquitoes away
and puffed perfect circles, O after O.
All signs of the vice have been blown away.

You called me one night with something to say.
Fags are the enemy. Smoking's the foe.
It's a rare sight now, the half-filled ashtray.

You struck a match. It's a price you will pay.
In the darkness I could see the tip glow.
All signs of the vice are hidden away.

The ashes were scattered where fireflies play.
I lit up a candle and watched you go.
I miss the sight now, the half-filled ashtray.
All signs of the vice are hidden away.

EVEN HIS MOTHER TOLD ME

TO RUN

Louise Norton

Blinded by your badness and your twilight looks,
subconscious salesman wearing only a trance,
with a pocket full of pills and a stitch in time.

Roll up, roll up for the time of your life.
The ghost train is waiting, down the track.
So,
pack up your thrills and fears in your cautious kitbag.

Even his mother told me to run.
I didn't listen, I didn't listen.
He might as well have been holding a gun.

I wish I'd listened.

Closed curtains know the score:
drawn into darkness,
can't find the door.

Trapped in a dark space,
wearing a different story
on my outside face.

Even his mother told me to run.
I didn't listen, I didn't listen.
He might as well have been holding a gun.

I wished I'd listened,
Wished I had listened.

THERE AND THEN

Jane MacKinnon

Where they loved, the comma, with its ragged wings,
danced drunken in the vine
and, atop the tawny grasses, the common blue
danced on and on, long after his blue eyes,
his cornflower blue eyes,
had closed in contented sleep.
She watched the skipper and the meadow brown
and stroked his dark brown hair,
streaked silver though he was still young.
In the lime tree, silver-washed fritillaries
whirled orange through the sunlit air,
bright precursors of autumn leaves.
These are the memories that skip and flutter through
        her mind.
These are the memories that she would like to catch
        and keep:
of a love that lasted through that time,
comma-punctuated – for love must breathe –
but without full stop

A FROWN FROM A LION

Barbara Kuessner Hughes

My small, clogged storeroom is a dismaying sight when I open the door and look inside.

But I must steel myself. How many years has it been since I shed any of the accretions of my long lifetime?

I reach a gnarled hand inside a box at the bottom of a cupboard and pull out my mother's old jewellery case. I've never used it. I don't particularly like it, and I've no-one to leave it to. Perhaps I ought to sell it?

No sooner have I pulled out the jewellery case than I realise what's lying beneath it. I gasp as my hand comes into contact with the faded red cover. How on earth can I have forgotten that I own this? And how strange it is – how an entire lifetime can flash back to one in an instant!

The schoolbook is a relic from the days when I believed truth and love to be everyone's defaults. Pressed into the pages between Byron and Shelley is a desiccated rose.

On that momentous night, Ted brandished the flower at me like a buccaneer's sword. I can still remember the heat in my cheeks when I accepted it.

I was the receptionist of a dancing school when Ted signed up to improve his already excellent dancing. I'd broken every rule of the establishment in order to see him. The principal of the school would have fired me immediately if he'd known. But I was simply overcome. Ted was so dashing! It was only much later that I realised how consciously he'd modelled himself on Errol Flynn.

He took me to see the musical *Carousel* for my twenty-first birthday. and afterwards, on our way home, we danced and sang 'June Is Bustin' Out All Over' and 'You'll Never Walk Alone' all the way to Trafalgar Square. It was a wintry night, and for once the air was clear of smog.

We were so desperate for colour and gaiety in that post-war rationed world. I remember everything as being monochrome, the food stodgy and scarce, the houses frigid, the clothing drab, the coffee like washing-up water.

A show in the West End was just the ticket, as we used to say. I was intoxicated in every way. I admit it: I'd had too much to drink that evening.

'This time next month, Phyllida, my darling,' Ted said, putting his arms around me, 'I shall be sweating like a pig and thinking of you – minus your winter woollies!' He squeezed my waist.

I'd been brought up rather genteelly, and I disliked the mention of sweating pigs, but I couldn't help smiling anyway. Ted's vitality, humour, confidence, dazzling dance moves, smooth neck and wavy brown hair flowed through my being ceaselessly. I hadn't known him very long, but he'd become as vital to me as my own bone marrow.

'Soon you'll be Mrs Laurie!' Ted declared. 'Mrs Phyllida Laurie has a ring to it, don't you think? I'll send for you soon as I'm settled. Ceylon! We'll have a smashing bungalow, first-class prospects, sunshine every day. Plenty of room for children. And when I've got some experience under my belt, we'll come back to Blighty and I'll start my own company.'

I beamed. I couldn't wait to introduce Ted to my parents. They'd slipped downwards so sharply in both morale and living standards since the War and the loss of my dear brother Robert. I was certain they'd appreciate Ted's drive, that he'd lift and enliven them.

We kissed in front of a lion statue. And then something curious happened. In those days Trafalgar Square hadn't been pedestrianised, and the cars were driving right past us. Perhaps it was simply a trick of Morris Oxford headlights, but I'd have sworn that the lion's bronze face was frowning. Now I wonder: was my subconscious warning me of danger?

I'm afraid to say that that night my virginity followed my heart. After Ted left my bedsit, I pressed the rose between the pages of my old school poetry book, feeling transformed forever.

Three months passed. Not a telegram, nor a single letter with a stamp showing an orchid, temple or Kandyan dancer.

Torment, indecision, dread of disgrace. I barely slept. I barely ate. I was sick all the time. I seriously considered throwing myself into the Thames or in front of a train. In the end I became immobilised: static, doom growing within me. It was only a matter of time before my secret came out.

One pea-souper Saturday afternoon, I was forcing myself to fry some Spam fritters when the doorbell rang.

'I'm Mrs Laurie – I think,' the wan, waifish caller declared. I hadn't the faintest idea who the woman was, but I felt sorry for her instantly. She'd have been pretty if she hadn't looked so hungry. Her face was pinched, her coat tatty. She seemed indignant, although not with me. 'Though God knows how many Mrs Lauries there are running about the place,' she went on.

I peered at her. I remember feeling baffled. 'I beg your pardon?' I happened to be holding a knife.

'It's no use stabbing me, love!' the woman said. 'I've done some detective work. Rotten bleeder's been leading a double life! Maybe even a triple one! And why stop there, eh? He was talking in his sleep, and then I found your letters hid inside a broken radiogram. Crafty devil! I thought, it's only fair to warn you.' I could feel my forehead frowning with the effort of trying to understand. I wasn't succeeding. 'But now he's scarpered. We shan't see him again.' Mrs Laurie pointed to her belly, round as a pear. 'Left me in the lurch, ain't he! I only hope he ain't done the same to you.'

That was it: at last I understood, and the world went like Vincent van Gogh's "The Starry Night", only dark and sinister. On my rapid descent towards the floor, my head met with the edge of the gas fire.

I came to in a hospital bed as a bandaged pariah, heart minced, abdomen uninhabited.

Aunt Edith was sitting by the bedside. Her touch

was tender, but her tone was taut. 'I'm relieved you're all right, Phyllida dear. But let us never speak of this again.'

'Mrs Laurie' had called a doctor and then disappeared. Perhaps she had something else to hide.

Oh, the shame, the shame. But I went on to make a life for myself.

I became the secretary to a school headmaster. He was demanding but fair, and he was kind enough not to ask uncomfortable questions. In fact, I became rather fond of Mr Prentice. But he already had a nice wife.

Several years later, I read in the newspaper that a certain 'Edward Mayhew' had been jailed for bigamy and fraud. I recognised Ted's photograph, and I cried. Tears of disappointment. Tears of relief that he couldn't hurt more poor trusting women. And I laughed, briefly, because he'd had his comeuppance. But I never fell in love like that again; I suppose my ability to trust had been too damaged.

I still manage the odd game of bridge, dahlia-growing, an occasional concert. A glass of sherry. I walk my terrier Roger daily, albeit slowly. Smoke curls cosily from my cottage chimney into the country sky. When I was younger, I'd bat away the odd proposal from my widower neighbour, Charles. *No thank you!*

Certain subjects make me go numb, but most of the time, contentment lies upon me like a faint golden dust. I'm an extremely fortunate woman: some chemical in my brain has rendered me one of nature's happy people.

But now I stare at the rose in my hand. If it hadn't been for this flower and everything that followed, perhaps I'd have married and had children like other women. Perhaps I'd have had someone to leave my mother's jewellery case to. I think of the son or daughter whom I never saw, never held, of his or her lost potential. They're barely even an outline, but they're still etched into me.

I feel a long moment of melancholy. Then I remind myself that evening pleasures await: a hot, scented bath, buttered crumpets and Mozart on the radio.

It was all so long ago.

The rose in my hand has crumbled into brittle pink dust before it reaches the bin.

5. Ties That Bind

WHERE THERE'S A WILL…

Sarah-Jane Reeve

Natalie found the will while we were stripping the dining room. The Last Will and Testament of Isobel Davidson. Dated 1975. Someone had hidden the documents under the floorboards. There were two old-fashioned floppy disks and a manila envelope with A4 sheets of paper inside.

We were renovating 43 Inverness Terrace, Ealing, the wreck of a house we had just bought. Natalie was seven months pregnant and on maternity leave, and we wanted to clean up and paint the house before baby Alice arrived. The scaffolding had gone up and the builders were expected but, full of enthusiasm, we were taking up the old carpet in the dining room ourselves and knocking through the kitchen wall. There Natalie found a loose floorboard, and beneath that the envelope.

Natalie being Natalie, my talented, curious, journalist wife couldn't help but wonder. 'We didn't buy the house from anyone called Davidson. So how long has the will been down there?' we speculated as we carried the old carpet out to the skip standing in the road.

'For heaven's sake, Nat, it's so old,' I said. 'It

would have been sorted out long ago. I say bin it.'

But later while on a tea break, we sat down and read the will. Another odd thing, it was handwritten and witnessed by a milkman, and a cleaner. But all Isobel's property, which was mostly the house and bank balance, were to be left to someone called Elena Aleksandrovna Stepanov. No explanation was given. No amount of money was mentioned. The executor was to be a local solicitor, Bradley & Morgan.

'Well, I would have thought they would have stored a copy of the will at the solicitors,' I said.

'Yes,' said Natalie, 'but why *hide* a will? Who was she hiding it from?'

'I don't know. Money-grubbing relatives?' I think at this point I picked up a sledgehammer. I was dying to knock down that wall. Natalie retreated to the hall.

'Maybe there were people who didn't want her leaving all her money to some Russian woman,' she said later, putting on the kettle.

'Probably,' I said. 'That's wills for you. People think "Who gets the money?" and "Why not me?" But these papers are so old that I can't imagine they will be relevant to anyone anymore.'

'Yes,' Natalie conceded reluctantly.

I told her straight, 'I know you like a mystery, Nat, but I can tell you one thing: neither Isobel Davidson or anyone else will be leaving *us* any money. We need to increase the value of this house and that means paying to renovate it.'

But Natalie was like a dog with a bone. Did Elena get her money? What was the Russian connection?

Natalie loved a puzzle, a trail of inquiry, as her bookcases showed; she had several shelves of detective stories.

'I have always wanted to write a book,' she said. 'Maybe this could be the basis of one. A little research wouldn't hurt. Perhaps the firm of solicitors mentioned in the will is still in business. They might still have a record of Isobel.'

'Don't you think we've got enough on? House? Baby?' I took out my irritation on the kitchen wall with the sledgehammer. I was going through the homemaking phase, this was our refuge away from the world.

But the next day Natalie internet-searched for the solicitors mentioned in the will, and found a Bradley & Son in Ealing, but not a Bradley & Morgan. She phoned and talked to the receptionist and found out that Mr Oliver Bradley had left Bradley and Morgan and set up his own business about thirty years ago. She made an appointment for the next day.

'How much will this cost?' I complained. 'We're spending a fortune on builders, you know.'

'Don't worry, it will come out of *my* money,' she reassured me.

We were shown in to the large, modern office of Oliver Bradley who looked middle-aged, prosperous and respectable. I felt foolish as Nat explained what had happened forty years ago and showed him the will and disks.

I was expecting frostiness but Bradley was intrigued: 'Well, this will was prepared in my father's time. That's Geoffrey Bradley when he used to be with Bradley & Morgan. But our archives go back sixty years and include some of the old Bradley & Morgan work. Of course, there is the issue of confidentiality, but it was a long time ago. I will look into it and give you a call.'

'But it is handwritten, isn't that odd?' asked Natalie.

'Well, it happens more often than you'd think,' said Bradley. 'A handwritten will is still valid if it is signed, dated and witnessed. But I will have to check whether there's a subsequent will in the file and how it was settled.'

'I must appear nosy but it was an odd thing to find – under the floor like that,' said Natalie. 'I just thought I should check it out.'

'Absolutely, I would have done exactly the same thing,' said Oliver, showing us out. He acted as if finding wills under the floor was completely normal.

Later that week, we went to the ante-natal classes at the church hall and met a couple who were to become our close friends. We were drinking tea after the session on Breathing in Labour when we got chatting to Mark and Hayley who were also renovating their house. Hayley was making waspish remarks about clearing Mark's stuff out of the garage so they could extend the kitchen. Apparently, Mark was in IT and was incapable of throwing away old computers, of which he had many.

Natalie grasped the opportunity like a shot: 'You don't happen to have a disk drive that could read my old floppy disks by any chance?' she said, and she told them the will under the floorboard story.

'Bring them round and I'll have a go,' Mark said. 'I love a mystery.'

So, the next evening we walked round the corner with a bottle of wine to *their* scaffolded house, and Mark and I disappeared into his garage to find the right disk drive.

Mark's garage was like a computer museum full of equipment. Some dated from the 1950s, he told me proudly. But with a bit of trial and error, he found the correct disk drive and printed out a sheaf of pages.

'Well, Pete, someone has saved some letters on to the disks. And some of them are in Russian.'

'Nothing to do with the will then?' Natalie asked when he showed her the papers.

'No. Well not as far as I can see, but I don't read Russian. What's this all about?' He laughed, 'Your Isobel Davidson: she wasn't a Russian spy, was she?'

Later that night we read the letters that were in English, written in 1975: Isobel was enquiring as to the whereabouts of the Stepanov family. The Russian letters looked like replies. Some were quite short, but one was long and seemed full of information.

Natalie felt frustrated. 'Now we are going to need a translator if we're going to get to the bottom of it. Who was Elena? Why did Isobel want to track down a Russian woman and leave her everything?'

'And how much is a translator going to cost?' I asked. 'File it away for when we're richer and have nothing to do.'

'Oh Pete, where's your sense of adventure? A Russian spy might have lived in our house. Why was the will hidden? Don't you find it intriguing? I want to know if Elena got her money.' Natalie was waving her arms around now.

'Well, I think you're getting carried away – we don't know she was a spy.' I grumped. 'It will all turn out to be something banal, you mark my words.'

The truth was, I liked having Natalie home on maternity leave. It meant I actually got to see her. Usually she was out at the office or chasing down some lead at all hours. She loved investigative journalism.

But Natalie wouldn't give up. Unable to sleep in the small hours she sat up in bed and started searching for translators on the internet, with no luck. The laptop light woke me up. Then she searched for Elena on some social media sites. Sure enough, she came up with several women called Elena Alexandrovna Stepanov but they were far too young to be *her* Elena. Some of the sites were in Russian of course which was no help. Then she found a chatroom about family tree research and left a message about tracking down Elena. By this time, I was annoyed and tired.

'You're becoming obsessed, Natalie,' I said, 'I'm no psychologist but perhaps thinking about this stuff is better for you than thinking about the birth.'

'No, you're certainly not a psychologist,' said Natalie. She snapped shut the laptop and pretended to go back to sleep.

The next evening, on my return from work, I found Natalie in a state of excitement.

'I've received a message from someone through

the chatroom! And there's a phone number.'

After a phone call we discovered that her name was Valeriya, she was Russian and newly arrived in the UK, and was doing family tree research of her own as she had English cousins. Natalie explained the Russian letters problem, and Valeriya volunteered to translate them.

Then I suggested Nat invite her to the pub with Mark and Hayley on the following Saturday night. I don't know why I got involved, I certainly regretted it later, but I thought at the time that the sooner we sorted out those letters, which I thought would be full of tedious stuff, then the sooner Natalie would lose interest.

Natalie was thrilled. Boring old Pete had redeemed himself. She gave me that admiring look which I hadn't seen for a while. I liked it.

So we all met up in the pub. And I think that what Valeriya read out to us that night was actually true. Valeriya was blonde and charming, quite a bit older than us, dressed smartly and worked in the city, she said. We all warmed to her.

We found a table and introduced everyone and had a light-hearted chat about family trees (Natalie suggested the Kew Records Office and the Imperial War Museum for Valeriya's own research).

Then Valeriya scribbled down a translation of the Russian letters, and read them to us, paraphrasing the parts that were difficult to translate. It was rather disjointed so in the end she summarised the main points.

'So, Isobel worked in Brussels at the British embassy in the 1970s,' she read. 'It is clear that she had a relationship with Yuri Stepanov, who was a Russian trade delegate.'

'Well, I've read spy stories and I think that "trade delegate" often meant "spy",' said Mark.

'Wow! That was a pretty dodgy relationship,' said Natalie.

'Maybe they were spying on each other,' I said.

'But who *is* Elena?' asked Mark.

'Elena Aleksandrovna Stepanov was their *daughter*,' said Valeriya.

'Of course. How could I have been so slow?' Natalie groaned.

Valeriya went on: 'It seems Isobel had to go to London for a couple of weeks for some meetings, so they decided that Yuri would take Elena to visit his mother in Moscow. It was arranged that Isobel would follow on later. But when she wrote and phoned Yuri from London to arrange the trip there was no reply. She returned to Brussels and went to the Russian embassy to check on his address in Moscow, but they were not able to provide it. They also said he was not due to return. So, Isobel went to Moscow to track down Yuri but with no success. Over the years she made more enquiries and advertised in Russian newspapers but heard nothing. The Russian embassy could not or would not help. Yuri never contacted her again.'

'Oh, my god. He took Elena away from her.' Natalie looked at me wide-eyed.

I must admit, I was shocked. Didn't Yuri and Isobel go through the pregnancy together like we were doing? And then the birth? They must have adored Elena when she was born. Mustn't they? This Yuri bloke was obviously a bastard.

'How could he?' whispered Hayley.

'It's so sad,' said Valeriya, 'but these were bad old communist days: my family could tell you awful stories. Maybe the authorities forced him to end his relationship with Isobel. It must have been terrible for her. But also for him.'

'And Isobel must have been in trouble with MI6,' Natalie said, 'I wonder what happened to her career.'

We all sat there glumly. Hayley looked up.

'So how old would Elena be now?' she asked.

'In her late forties maybe?' speculated Mark.

'As it was a long time ago, do you think there's anyone in the security services still living who would remember anything about Yuri, Isobel and Elena?' Natalie wondered.

Valeriya sighed, 'Look, I know you British are fascinated by all this spy stuff, but realistically, if Isobel couldn't find her partner and child then, how will you find them now, fifty years later? Believe me, Russia is a huge country. And names could have been changed.'

'I know, I know…' groaned Natalie. She appeared to think that her project was slipping away. I was pleased. It was going the way I planned.

'Well, that's the end of our little intrigue,' yawned Hayley.

At that they all sighed. Everyone got their coats and thanked Valeriya. I phoned her a taxi. Everyone said they would keep in touch.

'I'm just sorry it wasn't better news,' Valeriya said,

giving Natalie a hug.

Natalie and I went home, made some tea and sat by the fire.

'It's so sad,' I said, trying to sound sympathetic, 'about Isobel and her daughter.'

'I know – think of the years and years she went through wondering what happened to Elena. I feel we are so normal, and so lucky.' Natalie looked at me and squeezed my hand.

I grinned at her. 'Yes, lucky. And we are going to be *so busy*.'

The next day I got a call from Oliver Bradley which I thought really put the seal on it.

'Hi Pete, I went to the archive and looked at Isobel Davidson's file. There *was* an updated will, which referred to a trust for Elena. When Isobel died in the 1980s, my father somehow tracked down Elena and she received the money.'

'Ah, good – then case closed,' I said.

'Yes, case closed. I sorted it all out in five minutes, so I won't need to charge you. However, if you need help with anything else, feel free to call me.'

'That's decent of you, Oliver. Thanks,' I said.

I told Natalie the news.

'Well, that's the end of that,' she said.

We were pleased that Oliver did not charge us and agreed that when we were parents we would ask him to help us make our will, so Natalie filed his card away for later.

But then we were swept up in a whirlwind of events. That very night Natalie went into labour and Alice arrived, two weeks early. We just adored her.

She was perfect, she was ours and she was a joy. One day, Natalie held her and looked deeply into her blue eyes, and Alice looked right back. And Natalie said that Alice was a mystery, waiting to be explored.

And then late one night about four weeks later, I got a phone call from Valeriya. She wanted to meet me urgently. Right away, she said. It was 12.30 in the morning. Natalie and Alice were finally asleep. Thinking she was in some sort of trouble, I agreed. I walked around the corner at the end of our street and waited by the old post box like she told me to. Then Valeriya appeared.

'Well, is she still going on about Elena?' she asked.

'No – all forgotten,' I said. 'She is so in love with Alice, she's all she can think about. What's all this about? Why on earth have I got to meet you like this, Valeriya?'

'I'm warning you, Pete. The people I work for don't want any more investigations into Yuri and Elena, no more chatrooms, no more lawyers.'

'The people you work for? You're *warning me?*' I said. 'Is this some kind of joke?'

'Your lawyer started investigations in Russia,' persisted Valeriya. I was shocked. This was not the Valeriya we met in the pub, this was someone much, much harder.

'That was just us consulting Oliver Bradley about the will, he's just a local solicitor. I didn't know he investigated in Russia, we didn't ask him to. I thought he just got a file from his archives. Anyway, Elena got her money. The solicitors had a subsequent will. All is well. But, even if he did make some enquiries, why would Russian intelligence care about some British embassy worker's will from the 1970s? It's absurd!'

'It could be that Yuri was old KGB for one thing. Look, Pete, you and Natalie are nice people. But the new security services are not. You've been poking about in stuff you don't understand. You've just had a baby, get on with your lives and don't let some old will from someone you never knew jeopardise everything.'

I was furious. 'OK, OK! I recognise a threat when I hear it. This is appalling. You can bloody well tell them I have taken care of it.' I turned on my heel angrily and walked back to the house.

The next day I was still fuming. I found myself pacing up and down in our half-built kitchen. I still couldn't believe that conversation with Valeriya and felt really disturbed by it. Most of all I wanted to hear that Natalie and Oliver Bradley really had stopped investigating the will. But I had to tread lightly, Natalie was very tired. She was feeding Alice herself every four hours and was awake in the middle of the night, every night at the moment.

That evening we chatted while I made dinner. 'I was thinking,' I said, 'about our will.'

'Oh yes,' remembered Natalie. 'Well, we might as well see Oliver about it. But not now.'

'Yes, indeed. So, you haven't talked to him again about the Russian stuff then?'

Natalie yawned and looked fondly at Alice lying in her Moses basket. 'Goodness no, Pete, I think we've got quite enough on at the moment. Haven't we, Alice?'

I felt both relieved and confused. All I knew was

that Natalie and Alice had to come first. They had to be safe. Was Valeriya delusional or something? Who was she really?

A few days later I had the rare luxury of a day by myself. Natalie had taken Alice to see her mother and I decided to go for a pub lunch. I bought a newspaper and went to a pub on the common. On one side of the pub there were tables in booths separated by wooden screens. I chose one and opened my newspaper. Then I heard a familiar voice, and I realised that Oliver Bradley was in the booth next to mine.

'Well, how did it go?' he was asking someone.

A woman laughed: 'Very well. It's as we thought, they're just amateur sleuths. I told him the KGB story and Pete was scared to death. He is so gullible. I've been laughing about it all week. I don't think you will hear from him again.'

To my horror I realised that Oliver was talking to Valeriya – and she was talking about me. I felt a complete fool. Fortunately, because of the booths they could not see me.

'That's fantastic, Valeriya. Look, I've got your money,' said Bradley. I could hear the sound of something being passed across the table.

'But you're going to pay me more than this, Oliver,' said Valeriya, who wasn't laughing now. 'You've told me your secret and if you want me to keep it, you must keep *on* paying.'

There was silence as Oliver digested this speech. Then he spoke as if through clenched teeth: 'Keep your voice down, Valeriya. We made an agreement. I hope you're not going in for some half-baked blackmailing act.'

Valeriya went on regardless, 'Who knew Isobel was so rich? She lived in such a modest little house. You just keep paying me every month and I won't tell everyone that your father stole Elena Stepanov's inheritance, bought a big house, and set up the family business with it: a law practice. Bradley & Son. People expect solicitors to be trustworthy. What will people think when they read that it was built on theft?'

Oliver gave a sort of strangled laugh: 'It was four decades ago! I'm just making sure that nosy couple don't dig around anymore. But even if it got out there might just be a couple of embarrassing headlines then everyone would forget about it. After all, it was my father's crime. Not mine.'

Valeriya's voice changed, she was clearly very angry. 'Your father defrauded some poor kid. She may well be out there somewhere. I will tell everyone you hired me to cover it up.'

Now Oliver's voice was raised: 'Don't get above yourself, Valeriya, you're just an out of work actress!'

'Well, Oliver. I am about to play my greatest role. I will tell everyone that I *am* Elena Alexandrovna Stepanov come back to find her inheritance and see what happens to your business then. Who knows, maybe the real Elena will hear about it and show up. You need me to keep quiet. Pay up or else!'

I heard a crash as a glass hit the floor and Oliver left the booth and stormed out of the pub. I raised my newspaper to cover my face. Valeriya got up and followed him. I sat there stunned for a moment, and then gulped down my pint.

Then my phone beeped. It was Natalie sending me

a message. Attached was a beautiful photo of her and Alice. I looked at it proudly for a few minutes. I was just about to call her and tell her what had happened, and then I stopped.

I had stumbled upon fraud, blackmail, and spies, fake or otherwise. Natalie would go crazy for these details for her book. I could see it now. She would see it as a massive career move. The next few months would be taken up with investigations, she would be writing long into the night. She would go all out trying to find Elena. There might even be court cases. Any chance of a normal family life for us would be finished.

So, I decided not to tell her.

MOTHERSHIP

Louise Norton

Dark red rhythm ebbs and flows.
A whispering marimba
creeps into my ears.
A gushing, rushing soup of sounds.

I'm in here dancing with you,
my Mothership,
dancing with you.

A tincture of tone washes me tender,
symphonies of soul seep through my skin.
I float on a note and catch a sigh
and tumble in the gaps of silence.

FLOWER POWER

Jane MacKinnon

My brother was born to be a star.

I remember waiting for him to make his entrance, all through a hot, seemingly endless summer. My mother kept telling me what fun it would be to have a little boy. 'Feel how lively he is,' she said, placing my hand on her stomach. Kick, kick, kick – like some malevolent creature that would smash its way out and step from the shattered remains. My poor mother!

There's a photograph: Mother and me sitting on the garden swing in the shade of the elm tree. An elm tree! That's how long ago it was. Her with her dark hair tied back, her rounded tummy just noticeable under her loose yellow dress; me in dungarees with an orange striped T-shirt underneath, and a halo of blonde curls. I'm holding the perfect sphere of a dandelion seed head, my cheeks puffed and my lips puckered, ready to blow.

My mother taught me all the flower names and games. Buttercup – that name was obvious. 'Let's see if you like butter,' and she'd hold the glossy golden cup beneath my chin, so close that I giggled at the tickle I could nearly feel. Daisy – day's eye, because they closed up at night. I'd make a daisy-chain garland for her hair, or I'd pull off the petals, one by one. 'You love me, you love me not, you love me…' She must have known that most daisies have an odd number.

Once I picked an exception. 'You don't love me anymore,' I sulked.

Her hands rested across the bump that contained my brother. 'Perhaps you took two petals together, by accident.' I knew I hadn't.

I liked the dandelions best. Lion's teeth, it means, because the leaves are jagged, but I thought of them as dandy lions, proudly sporting their thick yellow manes. Fairy clocks – that's another name for them.

'One o'clock, two o'clock, three o'clock… Come on – one more puff and it will be time for tea.'

'What happens to them?' I asked, as the little parasols swirled high on the breeze.

'Some grow into new dandelions, some get eaten by the birds…'

'And the rest?'

'Oh, they take your dreams to heaven. If you go outside on a clear night, you can see them twinkling.'

One day she changed the game. 'How many weeks before your baby brother arrives?' I thought carefully and then blew as hard as I could. A veritable Milky Way of wishes rose to the sky. I looked back down at the limp stem in my hand and at the bald, misshapen head.

'Only one week?' laughed my mother. 'I wish!'

But the clock was right.

I never saw my brother. I'd blown him straight to heaven.

MEASLES 1980

Moyra Zaman

The Devil has come and he's taken my sunshine
    away;
his warning was brief as the temperature rose in the
    day.
In the heat of the night he wasted no time on his prey.
Mottled and crusted, the face of a child in dismay.

Laughter and life have been sealed in a menacing
    mask;
the young eyes are teased and retreat behind tears as
    they ask
why limbs are so limp and breathing a terrible task?
And hours trickle mucus, encasing the child in his
    cask.

The spirit by which I have known him is no longer
    there;
it's slipped through my fingers and silenced the space
    that we share.

But I know through my touch, through my song, he
    knows that I care.
He's too young to learn that this life can be very
    unfair.

In the wonder of sleep lie the weapons to fight the
    new day.
The fire on his forehead is quenched and the child is
    at play.
Then he coughs up the Devil who mocks my
    cowardly display
as Cambodia cries for her children far, far away.

MISSING WORDS

Moyra Zaman

Is it the way that I speak
or the way you fail to listen
that causes the gaps
where so much disappears?

The space from my lips to your ears
echoes with intonations
of misunderstanding;
even an intimate safety-net fails
to capture the gestures
with every turn of phrase.

Life's rich conversations sadly morph
to clamped communication –
a limited staccato,
now reduced to sound bites.

COFFEE

Barbara Kuessner Hughes

Margaret drinks coffee rarely; it's too emotive. She doesn't always want to return to Malaya in 1952. But today she's weary. She turns her teaspoon, thinking of other brown waters.

The sluggish ochre flow of a rainforest river. A gibbon whoops in an emerald tree above the boat. The outboard motor coughs. Sitting on Father's lap, Margaret fingers the craters of his bullet scars. His shirt is as damp as the humid air, his thin face lathed leaner by former torments.

Their home, the plantation manager's house by the river, is raised on pillars to exclude snakes and floodwaters. The corrugated-iron roof deafens when thundering rains crash. There is papaya for breakfast, curry for dinner.

Margaret enjoys following Father when he talks to the Tamil tappers. He smiles and jokes, unlike at home. She runs along solemn rows of grey-barked trees with diagonal cuts in their trunks, and cups to gather the sap.

A birthday party for three, cake with coffee icing.

Disgruntled with prettiness wasted, sociability stifled, Mother changes the record to Sinatra and slits her eyes disdainfully. The smoke from mosquito coils rises toward the sunset sky.

Rubber estates are oppressive, Mother says, the life lonely and dull.

Father frowns. It's a living. Bloody Hollywood fantasies! If you're bored, read! Just be happy! Didn't the War teach you anything? Or the Japanese? It's an Emergency! The Communists could shoot us dead tomorrow.

They sit in a coffee shop in town. Margaret tastes condensed milk and coffee, sweet and heavy in her mouth. There's a Chinese calendar with slashing scarlet calligraphy. A red roasted duck hangs up by its neck. She stares at a fly buzzing around the table as jagged words collide above her head.

Back in the now, Margaret pours more milk into her coffee to weaken its impact.

White slips and panties are spread out on her parents' bed. An empty suitcase awaits.

A few days later, a void opens and engulfs the whole house. Father drinks many dark and golden liquids. Never coffee.

She gazes at the white café tablecloth.

The letter comes in a white envelope, addressed to her, yet writing past and over her. No explanation that she has ever accepted, even now.

Father is withdrawn in the evenings, finally vanquished. His white shirt looms in the dusk as she looks out onto the veranda and tries to enliven him with her thoughts.

She seeks comfort in the kitchen, in the arms of Malay servants who murmur to her and pity her, and sometimes love her.

Time and the river flow ponderously past. Father sends her to a convent school. He doesn't concern himself with details.

Another piece of paper, a ticket, eventually bears her away to another life. A better life than she anticipated.

She looks up, wondering why she ever drinks coffee, why she doesn't try harder to evade these associations. She sees the father of her children, smiling at her as he strides through the door of the café.

MY MOTHER

Moyra Zaman

Resolutely, with a smile,
she heads off to the ironing pile.
In her home or as a guest,
the gift of ironing's her bequest.

The heavy board is heaved with grace,
eagerly ratcheted into place.
The iron has had its belly filled
with water, carefully distilled.

The tangled laundry's duly shaken,
grouped in bundles to be taken,
one by one, and spread exposed
upon the waiting ironing board.

Impatiently the iron is hissing,
reminding her that something's missing.
She turns to grasp the dampened cotton
handkerchiefs that she'd forgotten.

Then, without more hesitation,
she's right on task; her dedication
slowly smoothing out the creases
from the many stubborn pieces.

The scent of freshly laundered clothes
releases as the steam explodes
with puffs of mint and apple blossom
produced by movements light and lissom.

The swish of sheets is soon controlled
in every neat and measured fold.
Shirts are handled with precision,
collars first – that's her decision.

Nothing can escape her grasp
when she embarks upon this task.
She gathers all the underwear,
towels and socks and items rare.

In her hands the iron's her tool,
sculpting, pressing, warm or cool;
and, like a moving meditation,
rhythmically moulding her creation.

She fingers all the generations
in every garment's soft sensations,
smoothing their wrinkles as she goes,
transmitting love through ironing clothes.

THE UNFURLING

Barbara Kuessner Hughes

The minute my father's funeral was over, I turned to leave. I was hoping no-one would notice, but I wasn't fast enough.

'Oh, Robert! You're not going already, are you?' my Aunt Laura called out to me. Her voice sounded fractured and faded.

As I trudged across the leaf-sludged churchyard towards her, winding my way between gravestones, I remembered a word my mother had coined for such weather: drim. An amalgamation of dreary and grim. Along the way, I passed three of my five unfamiliar half-siblings, a row of chalky, tangerine-topped teenagers whom I'd never guess were my relatives if I hadn't been told. They regarded me with faces as blank as miserable sheets of paper. I wasn't sure they fully understood who I was. I tried to scrutinise them without being obvious. I'd never been this close to them before. Yes, I could see a sharpness around the jaw which reminded me of our father, Mick. Were the ribbons of DNA which we shared in common waving at one other, craving a family reunion? No. But I wished these sad-looking young people well. I'd come from our father Mick's first marriage, they'd sprung from his fourth. Standing in the church doorway was a rotund, scarlet-haired woman whom I'd been told was my half-sister Penny. I couldn't see any of my father's angularity about her. She turned in my direction, and I looked away quickly. We hadn't been introduced, and I didn't feel that I could face any more peculiar situations that day.

'Oh, Robert!' my aunt exclaimed when I got to her. For a moment I was afraid she'd sag against me. Comforting her wouldn't come naturally. Luckily, to my relief, she straightened up. But then I noticed how, beneath the brim of her black straw hat, Aunt Laura's face had collapsed, as though rain had oozed in beneath her skin. I felt an unwilling burst of sympathy for her. She'd idolised her rackety elder brother. The same sort of wilful blindness had characterised her entire life: she'd been too busy meditating to notice that her husband was a fraudster who was robbing her blind, too busy going on protest marches to see that her little girl was seriously ill, too busy making marmalade to notice that her son was turning into a criminal. Now my cousins were dead and in prison, respectively. *What a family,* I'd always thought, and done my best to steer clear.

'Blast and damn it!' Aunt Laura barked suddenly, making me jerk backwards. Then she added, in her usual apropos-of-nothing way, 'I suppose you are left-handed?'

'Erm, yes…?' I replied warily.

'I thought so. Hmm…' she murmured, puckering her lips. 'Which Hollywood movie star do you remind me of?'

'I've no idea.' I felt too damp and weary to be

flattered. 'Playing Twenty Questions, are we?' *She's still as mad as a bagful of bats,* I thought.

'You've got the same slim build and cheekbones and exquisite blue eyes as your dad! You're exactly like him!'

'I am?' Life frequently flummoxes me. *I'm the teetotal father of two grown-up sons,* I thought. *I've taught English at the same school for twenty years and been faithfully married to Jacqui for thirty years. And I married young. Yet I'm supposed to be like a high-spending, motor-racing, movie-star looking, cigar-smoking, gambling, five-times-married, boozing father of six? Grief has unhinged her.*

'He had good qualities,' Aunt Laura said stubbornly, seeing my clenched expression. 'Did you know, when our sister Sheila was dying, he helped to take care of her? You know how obsessed she was with the cinema?'

'Actually, I didn't.'

'He took her to the matinees at the Rex Cinema every afternoon, until she couldn't go anymore, and had to go into the hospice.'

'Really?' I said. I tried to keep my tone neutral.

'He was a very sensitive man, you know.'

Mainly towards himself, I thought, and trying not to think about the man whom I'd scarcely seen since I was eleven, I walked away. A month later the case arrived.

'These things are for you. Your dad had a great deal of time to think towards the end, and he knew he'd made a lot of mistakes,' Aunt Laura's note said. 'He spent the last two years of his life living in my spare room.'

He spent two years cramped up in his sister's tiny box room? I thought. *All that recklessness and alimony must have caught up with him.* But the thought of any human cooped up in what was not much more than a cupboard in my fruit loop of an aunt's house for two years was... Well. Somewhat reluctantly, I began to feel something. I pictured the man as I remembered him from photographs and a few vague memories, staring dolefully out of the window from his captivity. A few weeks passed. I ignored my curiosity, then finally surrendered. Inside the case was a notebook of mournful verses reflecting on the fact that womanising can lead to estrangement from one's children. I'd never known that he shared my desperate lack of talent for writing poetry. So, I did have something in common with him after all! Along with his other children, I was compared to receding waves on water, fragile saplings without the shelter of a larger forest, geese flying away over the horizon, never to return, and even – incredibly – little garden gnomes having a great time without the owner who'd arranged them in the garden. But instead of a sense of scorn, his verses gave me an obscure discomfort, like toothache fading out after a painkiller.

Feeling unsettled, I made myself some comforting tea in my tankard-sized mug. I can't abide dinky cups. Then I found the photograph. 'Last picture of Mick', the caption said, and the image made me put my mug down. It showed a gaunt, concave-cheeked, azure-eyed man clutching a giant mug of tea in his left hand and looking utterly bewildered by the universe around him.

6. Great Outdoors

MOONSTRUCK

Moyra Zaman

Dusk – the best – exhaling its low light across the furrows of the day. Releasing our shackles with a warm embrace, endorsing the fingering of expectant wine-filled glasses. All is well.

I drove westwards into the blazing sunset, unleashed and gaining speed, allowing Miles's trumpet to curdle my veins with 'Kind of Blue'. The blanket of fields lay exposed and defined by the clarity of the evening sky – a vast canvas freshly swept with vermillion brushstrokes.

My route took a turn. Suddenly from close behind my shoulder, I caught sight of a magnificent moon – huge and luminous it loomed low above a distant hedge and landed in my court. She was all mine. Transfixed, and like a selfish child, I claimed her for my own.

Thus, hypnotised and drawn under her spell, I was tempted to abandon the car. I felt the need to be outdoors and to be alone – with her. My emotions heaved like shifting tides, eager to feel the bite of the night air.

But life beckoned and this transient moment was quickly reduced to memory in the honking of a horn.

Angered now by interfering traffic and glaring headlights pathetically competing, I had to continue my journey – veering down leafy lanes where the trees teased and the moon flirted in between.

When she reappeared, her glow had gone. I felt saddened and cheated to see that misty streaks of cloud had now seized her, dressing her in wan apparel and obliterating her shining soul. I was hopeful that on our next encounter, she would be released and returned to her former glory.

On arriving at my destination, I stepped out of the car to look for her. There she was – elevated, beautifully formed but now aloof and distant – the magnetism gone. But a bond had been made. I stood and quietly acknowledged her steady gaze knowing that she would always be there, looking out for me.

The following day the radio announcer reduced my moment to a mere spectacle, informing the world that a 'super moon' had appeared for the first time in seventy years. He encouraged everyone to hunt her down – to tick the box. Did they not know I had beaten them to it? I'd had my moment, my surprise visitation, my intimate encounter! The moon had found me – the chosen one – and forever more we'll be watching and winking into the night.

THE OPPORTUNIST

Moyra Zaman

Dawn finds him there,
first to the table
defiantly scaling
the slippery pole.
In a flash he's contorted
inverted and hanging
determinedly gripping
the feeder and gnawing;
nibbling the nuts
with vigorous fury,
cheek-pouches expanding
his belly ignored.
Momentarily stilled
by intrusive rustling,
ears pricked, eyes darting,
jaws pausing, heart pounds:
held in a vice, a snapshot in time,
this mere flop of fur
plummeting to the ground.
Bouncing for cover,
audacious and deft,
a flick of the tail,
pleased with his theft.

THE ONE THAT GOT AWAY

Pat Abercromby

Giddily flirting with the ripples, she darts and twists, her rainbow mantle iridescent in the deep, clear, cold stream.

She catches a glimpse of the looming shadow above her, feels the vibration of the teasing morsel gliding nearer, sees the tempting glint of pink and yellow fronds coming ever closer. She dives down, turns, then flashing upwards, leaps out in mocking joy, her bright silver gleaming in the shafts of dappling sunlight. Her body curls and curves downwards, cutting knife-like through the crystal surface, leaving behind the merest, rippling wake.

Enraged, the fisherman stirs up the clear water with a stick, clouding the surface with muddy brown silt.

Blinded, she circles in a panic, open mouthed, seeking comfort from the texture of the treacherous mayfly. The hook digs cruelly into the soft flesh of her cheek. Frantically, she dives, torpedoing away from the torment but the relentless tugging is dragging her back. Desperately twisting and turning trying to release herself, her heart is near to bursting as she is dragged out of the water. Pressure on her gills as the hook is pulled from her cheek. She flaps her tail weakly, helplessly, her life force slowly draining away.

Then Zeus opens the heavens like never before, a churning, swirling deluge of water rushes along, claiming everything in its path. The fisherman jumps back in alarm as the water floods over the edge of the stream. The trout rolls and tumbles into the torrent. With a flick of her silver tail, she is gone.

The fisherman retreats, soaked, boots squelching and loudly cursing. 'Scheisse! Verdammt Forelle!'

With a nod to Schubart, Lyricist

EVERYONE LOVES A DUCKLING

Jane MacKinnon

Cute clockwork bundles of soft yellow fluff –
the blonde duck on our pond, now proud matron,
has hatched twelve ducklings. That's more than enough
to sustain the mallard population.

At daybreak a startled grey heron lifts
slowly, hauling its breakfasted weight.
The balance of duck life suddenly shifts.
The heron has eaten: ate equals eight.

By moonlight fat brush follows the fox
into the shadows. I cannot be sure
what it feeds to its cubs deep in the copse.
By morning the ducklings are down to four.

Swaggering drakes descend in formation –
all glossy green heads, murderous bills –
each one obsessed with the replication
of its own genes. They come ready to kill.

The duck swims and dabbles, outwardly calm
beside the drake with the deadliest beak.
Does she feel the loss or recall the harm
done to her brood? All twelve. Gone. In one week.

STORM OVER DARTMOUTH

Sarah-Jane Reeve

As I looked across the rooftops of the town
we were invaded.
Clouds grasped our cloak of hills,
rain spattered spitefully across our windows,
far houses on the bay were blurred,
and the bright blue light of the estuary
was extinguished.
The town's palette was washed into grey.

With war-like timpani
wind persecuted raving trees
and flung their branches against verandas.
Tormented flags on the church surrendered
and babies, all, the seagulls cried and cried.

One bird and her brown-feathered chick
shivered on the slick wet roof
in a chimney lee.
The child hungrily peeped and bobbed
but mother flattened herself against the slates

and looked to the distance.
The people are inside and hatches are battened.
No spilt food today.
The wind betrays us
go aloft and we'll be blown apart and away.

But even winds tire.
Far below tiny bell ringers dared the deluge
and ran to the church to resist
the drowning of the town.
The chimes sang and signalled,
sallied and rallied
and blue fought with grey in the bay.

In disarray the town finds the light.
And as the last bell says, 'Enough,'
the storm drives back to sea
and the seagulls shriek in triumph.

DEAD MEAT

Louise Norton

Doors crash open, hit by icy air.
A rush and a crush, herded along;
a sharp shock to my head
and I'm gone.

Dead meat now, no going back.
My shape once whole, lies in pieces.
Same cells remain
only now I'm wrapped in cellophane.

Grabbed by a hand from a supermarket shelf,
plonked in a basket with other foodstuff,
taken away to a warm human home
and into a fridge, cold and alone.

Prised from my packaging, slapped in a pan,
my sizzling flesh composed to taste:
served up à la bovine,
washed down with a glass of wine.

Shunted along in this relentless place,
pummelled, puréed and processed.
The best of me kept, the rest discarded
and swept away.

Down, down to the sewers I go –
heaps of muck everywhere,
noxious fumes and toxic gasses
stuck in the stink of my own remains.

I used to be called Blossom.

DRY SEASON

Moyra Zaman

I loiter in stubble,
shrivelled and parched,
amidst litter blown
like scattered leaves.

Seeking shade, I crouch
by wizened trees,
naked protrusions
biding their time.

A whirlwind of dust
pin-pricks its way
to my face,
gritting my eyes,
silencing my throat.

I have no voice
against the elements;
my dry breath,
a shallow reminder
of who I am.

Far away I see
a lone jacaranda –
its resilient flourish,
a purple cloud of hope.

And so, I know
my time will come,
surely, inevitably;
it's just not yet my season.

Zambia September 2019

URBAN JUNGLE

Moyra Zaman

Intrepid explorer, stepping out bravely,
following routes unfamiliar and slow;
cautiously stepping, avoiding excreta,
booting the leaves of litter below.

My gaze turns the corner, alerted by horns:
a stampede of metal is funnelled my way.
Flashing eyes are distorted, pollution is snorted,
I head for the alley, rock cobbled and grey.

A carcass of concrete is shedding its pelt –
Old news, old news, now stripped and misspelt.

I fall into step with a herd of commuters,
crossing the river of traffic in flow.
Hear squawking of brakes and the clamour of engines
revving impatiently, waiting to go.

Pass human cocoons morphing in doorways,
while buskers are burrowing deep underground.
Protesters are howling and fat cats are prowling
in streets where the red lights and short skirts are found.

The grey squad of pigeons patrols underfoot,
reinforcements are perched on the high wire en route.

Now wearily wandering, lured by the sirens
An accident imminent? Criminal intent?
The jungle is restless with self-righteous rumours,
billboards are flashing 'dissent and prevent!'

A green streak of parakeets screeches above
sartorial catwalks oblivious below.
Cash tills are reckoning but savannahs are
beckoning…
enough of the creepers and peepers on show.

Nature is tugging the cuff of my sleeve.
This is my signal – I'm ready to leave.

DISTANCE

Jane MacKinnon

The brightness of birdsong,
the far-away baa-ing of sheep –
these are the sounds that wake me from,
and lull me into, sleep.

And I sink back and think:
All's well with the world.

But the feathered breast swells to threaten a fight,
and the bleats are from dams
who have lost their lambs
and cry through the night.

These creatures call through worry and grief,
yet as I listen, I feel at peace.

Is there another self, distant in the universe,
who hears with joy the diverse noise rising from
      our earth?
The chit-chat chatter of the battle guns,
sweet keening of those who sob for their sons.

Does she, like me, sink back and think:
'All's well with the world'?

And when our planet is no more –
light years ahead of where we are –
will my soul, hear its dying roar
and smile at the brilliance of our falling star?

Will she, like me, sink back and think:
'All's well with the world'?

THE INNER HELMSMAN

Anne Silk

Senses set firm – wise controller of this mighty ship,
your inner helmsman always seeking.

Eyes take in the light, the dark, here subtle shadows,
there the hovering dove close by.

Two million light-years far above, you spy Andromeda.
Hands grasp the wheel – you know the path of time.

Ears hear the roaring gales of Nature,
the gentle lap of waves against the hull.

Leaping dolphins seek clear air above
then dive to rolling deeps.

Senses – themselves the orchestra –
Link Earth and Eternity in perfect harmony.

Darwin, Descartes and Paracelsus – three wise men –
described their art.
Now rightly permeating all, is science.

The compass spins, as do the molecules within
      the brain.
Where does it point? No one yet knows.

Ponder on Infinity, vast, impenetrable.
The Universe unbounded – yet to be explored.

DANCE THE TULIP

Moyra Zaman

Dance the tulip, stem the sway,
(the vase cannot contain you).
Sleek and supple, seeking light,
with random rhythms, taut delight;
poised in flowing transformations
choreographed anew each day.

Dance your flames of red and yellow,
kindling ancient arabesques,
configuring curves in rigid rooms,
in stagnant corners, changing tunes,
adopting Monet as your muse,
confusing coloured brushstrokes grow.

Unlike the screw's reliant thread –
beneath its head, a twisting groove –
your path's untethered, wild and free.
You dance so optimistically,
until, exhausted, petals fall
from knotted noose and bowing head.

7. Journeys

THE LONG WALK

Jane MacKinnon

Take off those heavy boots, my friend,
and empty out the desert sand.
Your long, hard march is at an end.

Peel off those sweat-soaked socks that cling
despite the holes too big to mend.
Shed them as a snake will shed old skin.

Rip off that frayed Elastoplast:
the heel is no longer bleeding.
The need for bandages is past.

Brush off the dirt whose chafing grit
burst blisters that had formed so fast
and caused more pain than you admit.

Here is cool water in the shade
to bathe your sore, new-bared feet. Sit
until the aches begin to fade

then stand. Feel the tickling grass – and
mark the imprint of every blade
upon your soles. Here is your land.

BROKEN NAILS

Kim Abercromby

I walk for miles on broken nails,
catch a glimpse beyond this playground waste,
wonder what it's like to live that way.
Beyond the tin top roofs I gaze.
Out there I see colour, it's far away,
I hear children's laughter way out there.

One small act of kindness made my day.
Someone passing threw a bag my way.
Inside a pair of shoes they gave
sprawled before me like a king they lay.
On this day a little softer, no broken nails,
I'll run a little faster on this day.

This king appears among the crowd
Hungry eyes see me, I look down,
hold my breath, face to the ground.
They stole my shoes and broke my crown.
Down here I see nothing
but broken nails.

I'd run if I could,
there's no escape.
And I'd cry but it's no use,
It's far too late.
There's no one to hear me,
in this whole place.

There nothing to hear me but broken nails.

LIFE'S TRAJECTORY

Moyra Zaman

I arrived, snowbound
lovingly nurtured in cotton wool
and smiling – sensitively reared.
Soon questioning beyond
the black and white responses,
suffocating softly, waiting for wild winds
to blow the windows wide.

Spreading my wings,
I soared, I saw through open doors,
filled my head with far off lands
and coloured threads.
I wove my tale in sunshine
and happily, looking inwards,
set my compass homeward bound.

THE CASE OF THE MISSING GIRL

Jane MacKinnon

You read this sort of stuff in the Sunday tabloids: a young girl found, after God knows how many years, stuffed into an improbably small suitcase; the killer returning to the victim. No smell of decay, not now – it must be half a century ago at least, judging by the thickness of the dust – and no signs of a struggle. I push at the dust with an old tissue and wipe my grubby hands on my jeans, suddenly engulfed by regret and sadness about what had happened. I must have suffocated her, slowly, slowly, suffocated her. Yet no-one reported her missing. Did anyone even notice she had gone?

The last certain memory is of her standing at the bus stop, shiny hair – brown, touched by the sun so that in some light it looks blonde – hanging below her shoulders. She's wearing a home-made mini dress with a geometric orange and yellow print.

'Is it too bright?' she'd asked anxiously as the stallholder measured off two yards of the fabric.

'Oh, you're young, you can wear anything,' was the reply.

That's true, though those are not the best colours for her. No jewellery. Bare-legged. I can't describe her shoes: they're hidden behind her suitcase. *This* suitcase, the one I've just found. A Revelation – a bit of irony there, considering what it has concealed for so long – in heavy red vinyl with strong clasps. Good quality. The right size for a weekend away. Where is she going? She looks apprehensive rather than excited and, I realise now, vulnerable.

The bus arrives – a Greenline single decker. The only free seats are at the back with the smokers, all men. She's worried now and sits down by a window, naively leaving the aisle seat next to her vacant.

I can't remember what happens next, or how I'm suddenly fifty years older.

I look again at the small red suitcase, lying on the floor, empty save for this lingering ghost of my youth.

The case looks quite smart in a retro chic sort of way. Perhaps I'll start using it.

CLEARING THE MIND

Jane MacKinnon

Memo to self: put affairs in order,
the deadly boring task that we all dread –
for who is not an inveterate hoarder
of paperwork? There are drawerfuls to shred:
statements, receipts from a lifetime ago,
records of income and expenditure.
So much money spent, so little to show.
Just proof, perhaps, that there was a career.
Bookings for best-forgotten foreign trips;
A fortune on clothes in dubious taste
(a dress to impress with too many zips);
brand new appliances, broken, replaced.

Shred all evidence and let memory
be the kind keeper of identity.

FABRIC OF LIFE

Jane MacKinnon

When I was a country child,
I gathered the lambs' wool tufts
that blew on the briar and caught on the haw.
I took them home and combed them into puffs –
warmth for a nest box, or stuffing for a teddy's paw.

When I was a country girl,
I gathered wool to spin a yarn;
never long or strong enough to knit
a plain tale or cast a purl.
Instead, I used the threads to darn
holes in my story where truth didn't fit.

When I was a country bride,
I gathered wool to weave
a dream with warp so strong and weft so fine.
I watched the lovely cloth unfurl
and spread its hope across my bed.
With lamb-like trust, I did believe
that all I wished for would be mine.

When I was a country wife
I gathered each loose end
and neatly tucked it, thread by thread,
into the fray of my worsted life.
All the dreams had been blown wide.
There was no making then – just make do and mend.

Now I am much older.
I pull time's fabric like a shawl
about my bony shoulders,
grateful that its warmth will one day be my pall;
and edges of my early selves will all be reconciled.

8. The Bright Side

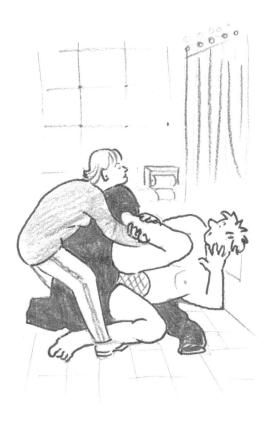

WE'D KNOWN EACH OTHER FIVE MINUTES

Libby Evans

My daughter was selling her ex-boyfriend's wetsuit. He was a slim young man, now long gone and living in America.

A strong athletic guy came to try it on. He looked every inch a surfer – a likely buyer.

I showed him into the downstairs loo and shower room to try it on and joined my mother and daughter in the kitchen to enjoy our pot of tea.

'Hello,' came the voice from the shower room.

'Hello,' we chorused back.

'Is here a man in the house?'

'No,' I shouted. 'Why?'

'I can't get it off,' came the reply.

Long pause – we stopped sipping tea and looked at one another.

'I'm broad-minded,' I offered and went in.

He was sitting on the loo with the suit round his ankles and very old Aertex underpants keeping his act together.

This is the conversation as heard from the kitchen:

'How about if I jerk it quickly? Shall we twist and pull? Some oil might help. We might have to cut it off.'

By this time, he had gone pink all over, was on the floor, and the old Aertex pants had given up their task and the contents had fallen out.

'I'll just leave you to tidy a little,' I coughed and escaped to the kitchen where my daughter was sliding down the wall hysterically and my dear old mother was saying, 'What's going on? My tea's gone cold.'

I returned to the scrum. He had somehow managed to free himself of the wet suit.

'Something to tell them down the pub,' I joked and left him to dress.

He emerged from the shower room and made a beeline for the front door.

'Shall you be buying it?'

THE ACCIDENT

Moyra Zaman

And here I am
bloody-nosed, shoulder cringing,
wrist slung painfully, wryly warning me
I'm no spring chick.
Heed your age, walk with a stick.
No way, no way.
I'll be fine in a day… or two… or maybe three.
Oh, gammy knee,
don't laugh at me.
I enjoyed my trip
till landing splat, completely flat,
deflated.
Hey-ho, I'll have to go
to Santiago in my mind,
another dream to leave behind.
Hip without the hop,
that's my lot these days.
Remember all those crazy haunts
frequented by my nimble joints?
My dance is now a paltry sway.
I never thought I'd be this way.

ON CONTEMPLATING A NEW EXERCISE REGIME

Jane MacKinnon

I'd like to thank my mom – oops! – wrong speech. I'd like to thank William Shakespeare, The Book of Common Prayer, John Dryden, TS Eliot and the Bible.

'O! That this too, too flabby flesh would melt,
thaw, and resolve itself as six-pack firm;
or that the gods of fashion had not fix'd
'gainst faces framed with rippling double chins.
Spare tyres and bulging thighs are just not 'in'.
How weary, stale and flat seem all my shoes,
worn down by the heaviness of my form.
Fie on it! O fie! I must join a gym.
Like an unweeded garden gone to seed
I'm gross in nature. That it should come to this!
Just two raspb'rry milkshakes, nay, not so much,
each day; a can of Coke; a chocolate bar;
a hamburger in a sesame bun.
And yet, within a month, I was undone!

For I have left undone those things which I ought to
    have done (the skipping rope is yet unwound)
and eaten those things which I ought not to have
    eaten (sticky toffees by the pound).

Better go running and get health free
than pay the gym's hefty membership fee.
The wise, is they have some weight to lose,
start at the bottom with new training shoes.

But I grow old... I grow old...
I shall wear the bottoms of my joggers rolled.
I shall dye my hair – do I dare? – a shade of peach.
But I cannot wear Lycra ™ and walk upon the beach.
I've heard the youths laughing, each to each;
I think that they are laughing at me.

And the ripples of laughter were made rippling flesh.

IMAGINE

Moyra Zaman

When I was child
I danced with the stars,
I hitched to the moon
and travelled to Mars.

I talked to the sea
and it waved me a roar.
I swam to an island
by the time I was four.

I fell out of the window
whilst trying to fly;
I'd forgotten my wings
which I'd left out to dry.

I dressed like my friend
and she dressed as me;
we both fooled our mothers
when we went home for tea.

I eyeballed a lion
when I went to the zoo,
and it opened its jaws
when I said, 'How are you?'

I followed a rainbow
and bathed in its gold,
then painted my room
with its colours, so bold.

Mm… Now that I'm older
It's all rather vague,
but I'm sure I remember
when I had the plague.

LOVE AT FIRST SIGHT

Jane MacKinnon

French. Dark hair, brown eyes, deep dimples and a twitch of sensuality in his smile. Gorgeous… and sitting opposite *her*, gazing deep into her eyes. Deep, and deeper, uncovering secrets that she didn't know she had.

'Jan-ette,' he began, and she thought how much prettier her name sounded with the first letter softened and the emphasis on the second syllable. 'Eet 'as to 'appen. Eet ees inevit-A-ble.' He put the stress on the fourth syllable and the word did, indeed, seem to carry the force of destiny. Her mouth dried and her palms felt clammy. She fumbled nervously for her glasses and dropped them on the floor. How many pairs had she ruined like this? Michel waited patiently as she tried to compose herself.

'Come Friday evening.' Michel took her hand and smiled. She nodded

And so she found herself in a shabby part of the city, lying on a narrow bed, her head gently cradled and Michel looking down at her intently.

'You are perfect like that. Don't move.'

This is what I want, she told herself as she felt the light pressure of his fingers… deft, expert. She wasn't the first, she knew. He was – of course – highly skilled.

Afterwards, she obediently ate the meal that was put in front of her although she could taste nothing and, if she were honest, she was feeling a bit sick. Then: 'I'll call a cab. You must go home now. Things will be clearer in the morning. You will come again on Wednesday?' It wasn't a question. He knew she would.

She was dazzled. Outside, cascades of white, yellow, red and green hung motionless in the night sky. Every shop sign, headlamp and traffic signal was surrounded by a halo of shattered light. She was travelling, blind as love, through a slow motion fireworks display.

She pulled out her phone and squinted at the time. She had to call her husband, tell him which train to meet. She'd be very late. She felt a twinge of guilt.

But Michel was right. She *did* see things more clearly in the morning and she knew she couldn't stop now. This beautiful man had given her something wonderful, something so liberating, something that, at her age, she never believed she'd experience again.

Sure enough, on Wednesday she was there, sitting opposite him, letting him gaze, once again, deep into her eyes.

'I am ver' 'appy,' he said. 'Are you 'appy?'

'Yes,' she said firmly. No nerves now.

'I'm pleased. So I see you tomorrow evening.' He gave her that irresistible smile. 'And I will operate on the other eye.'

She'd already thrown her glasses away.

EASY CARE

Jane MacKinnon

As we grow older, so we will
join the ranks of those who spill.
Poured tea will nearly meet the cup
(just use a sleeve to mop it up);
the brimming spoon will reach the lips
half empty. The resultant drips,
in all of their disturbing hues,
will decorate our clothes and shoes.

No more 'designer' this or that
(though one could risk a stylish hat).
It doesn't matter what we wear
if the label says 'easy-care'.

FROM ALL DIRECTIONS

Autobiographical poems inspired by

'I come from' *by Robert Seatter*

Moyra Zaman

I come from a merry mobile home
harnessed in Scotland,
living everywhere else…
with the sound of my voice a self-conscious echo,
of Glaswegian glue holding memories secure:
misty-eyed islands, melancholy drones,
guttural laughter and rattling of trams,
kilts, strathspeys and church on Sunday,
imperial sermons, roast dinner in the wings.

I come from exotic foreign lands
like Tyneside and distant Empire days,
land of hope and glory, pantos and maypoles…
The lure of unknowns,
pubescence, daft Jimmy,
and, oh, for a wall to play 2-ball
and a rope to go skipping through a childhood of
      wild waves,
chase and kiss playtimes
and you'll get wronged for that!

I come from Manchester's heatwave:
water from the pump,
dried out rose-beds weighted with clay
and wild weeds – the punishment plot!
I come from a garden of stillness, studying at dawn,

exams weaving through the coy, teen time,
the youth group, the jukebox, the Dansette in
    the corner.
Billy Graham, West Side Story, Man Uni victorious,
battle cries of the Beatles, the city furore.

I come from Southampton –
The rawness recedes.
A temperate climate, tea parties and tennis,
polite conversations, complacent wellbeing.
(The Anderson Shelter clogged up and forgotten.)
The dregs of the day spill out in the kitchen,
a retreat for the senses, a welcoming space,
where passions are kindled and dreams can unfold.
Discussions arise and decisions are made.

I come from a need to return to my roots,
slipping in through the back door, adapting with ease
to heather and folk songs, 'Jimmy Riddle' and all…
Where colourful banter unzips all pretences,
life's proudly debated and sung from the heart;
but the lure of the mountains and screel of the pipes
can no longer ground me with tartan delights.
My baggage has changed me to 'voyeur at home'
so I come from a world where I'm destined to roam.

Sarah-Jane Reeve

I come from the 1970s,
from 1950s working parents,
who never had it so good.
Where dads waited for slam-door trains
in the suburban bubble.

I come from grammar school hats and stripy scarves,
boys with long hair, girls with short skirts,
steamed up school buses,
purple flares and Walnut Whips
and *Jackie*'s fashion tips.

I knew a bloke who knew a bloke
who was at school with someone famous.
I come from a generation
who all knew boys in a band
until Blondie.

I come from confirmation classes,
while Mum worshipped Delia Smith.
I come from A-Level Shakespeare,
unaware of Belfast's tragedy
on colour TV.

I come from helping Mum:
proudly unliberated and working.
Vacuum the shag-pile carpet.
Iron Dad's shirts.
And babysit for Aunty Jo.

I come from studying
by Miners' Strike candlelight.
Articulating for elocution lessons
while telly Vietnam
droned on.

I come from discontented winters.
Too young to join the dots,
inoculated with naivety.
I looped the loop with Spirograph
and still the strikes went on.

I come from TV in the corner
news, and more bad news
tugging vainly at complacency.
Rising aspirations, galloping inflation,
we all joined the bourgeoisie.

Louise Norton

I come from a breath
that lives in a sigh,
released from a womb
in Glasgow.

A gathering beyond
hosts a hearty party,
all DNA invited.
I grab my fair share.

Elements collide, coincide,
a splinter off a star
moonbeams dance
a distant yell…

I appear, to be me.

And then…

I became a conscientious
observer.

Pat Abercromby

The psychic said I came from a seven-star
    constellation.
Child of Taurus, a Celtic alien.
Wouldn't surprise me at all.

Didn't fit with the mean city streets,
in ancient times a green hollow.
Glasgow town where the sparrows cough,
huddled in bare grey-grimed branches.

Unwilling bridesmaid in tight peach satin:
Winter skin in wrong spring colours.
Haste ye to Scotia's still, deep lochs,
Ben Nevis limned in silver snow.
Seduced by its beauty, deflowered, transcended…

Run away, run away from the ties that bind.
Foreign shores beguile and charm, not for long.
Seeking some normality, calling it home.

Now ambitions, passions, all unfurl,
carelessness of caring takes its toll.
Seven sisters reclaim, I hear them call –

Shall I return to my star constellation?

Jane MacKinnon

I come from the futile holiday pursuit
of catching a seagull in mid-flight,
in perfect focus, black and white.
Then, minutely measured alchemy:
transmutation of film to photograph,
in the dark and under orange light.
There is an album full of sharp-eyed gulls.
Not one is in the air.

I come from unlabelled sunsets,
taken who knows where.
There are two hundred perfect slides
of backlit clouds and fiery skies,
captured before the darkness fell
and the lights of passion dimmed and died.

I come from the silence that filled the room
when the piano stopped,
when friends were not allowed
and the radio was turned off
by the husk of a man
who could not cope with loss.

He gave me silence and darkness
I love their contradictions,
In silence I can hear so much;
the wakening birds, the owl at dusk.
As night thickens, I can see
darkness, like snow, takes the unsightly,
blurs it lightly with beauty of its own.
Memories out of focus.

Contributors

Pat Abercromby has an eclectic background: she started in medical research, followed by founding a medical sales recruiting company in the UK. Next came freelance journalism and radio broadcasting in Saudi Arabia where she lived for six years, followed by six more years of family life in other overseas countries. Back in the UK she retrained in complementary therapies and teaching. Since 2017 she has published two novels, *Just One Life* and *The Knife Edge*. She lives in Buckinghamshire, has two daughters and three grandchildren.

Jane MacKinnon spent her working life in England and Australia as a writer, subeditor and editor for a variety of magazines, ranging from *Here's Health* (keep taking the kelp) to *Good Housekeeping*. Now retired, she writes for pleasure, walks the dog, organises a shambolic book club and volunteers for the Home Library Service. She lives in Buckinghamshire with her husband and the dog.

Sarah-Jane Reeve began her career in the publishing world working on film magazines, before moving on to books. She has since worked in book promotion, editorial, production and retail and has been a publishing freelancer for many years. Sarah enjoys writing creatively and researching the lives of her grandparents during the 1930s and 1940s, which included numerous overseas postings. An avid traveller and lover of Japanese food, she now lives in Berkshire with her husband and two daughters.

Moyra Zaman was born in Glasgow, spent much of her life travelling and volunteering abroad. Originally a research biochemist she later trained in fine art and textile design. After working as a colour consultant for the interior design market, she taught art at Chesham Grammar School for twenty years. Here she promoted global education gaining the school the International School Award, led World Challenge expeditions and developed a partnership in Ghana. Now retired she is a Trustee of the charity Workaid, teaches yoga and writes whenever she can. She lives in Amersham and is married with two sons and two grandsons.

Louise Norton was born in Glasgow. She worked as a professional dancer and choreographer for over twenty years, enjoying a diverse career. Dancing cabaret in Scotland, Italy, Malta and Tehran. Worked with Scottish Ballet for a season. A soloist with the Irish Ballet Company. Danced with South Africa's first multiracial contemporary company, 'Jazzart' Cape Town. And with 'Napac' Dance Company in Durban. Returned to the UK, qualified as a reflexologist. Started singing at sixty, along with a wee slice of creative writing. Tap dancing followed a little later… Now singing, writing songs and playing with words. A proud mother and grandmother living in Beaconsfield.

Barbara Kuessner Hughes was born in Malaysia, grew up there and in Singapore, and now lives in Hertfordshire with her family. She is particularly keen on writing short fiction and drama, and has had work published by Flash 500, Reflex Fiction, Three Drops From a Cauldron, Mojave Heart Review and other publications.

Libby Evans studied art and design at Hull Art College in the 1950s, then came south to design packaging at Goya (cosmetics). Whilst raising a family and over several decades, she has done a variety of freelance art projects including sculpture. For the last five years she has taught art to small groups including members of U3A. She loves to see people learning a new experience. She self-published her first book of illustrated stories titled *Malaprops Ad Lib* and has designed book covers for Pat Abercromby.

Kim Abercromby is a recently qualified counsellor with a background in the field of body work. Her passion for songwriting started after the birth of her first child, however she has been writing poetry from a young age. As soon as she learned a few chords on the guitar, she discovered that songwriting came naturally to her. This creative outlet helps her to channel inner feelings and reflections and it is always her hope that her lyrics may reach and move others.

Anne Silk is a former clinician who developed an international contact lens consultancy. Since retiring she has forged a second career in neuroscience and the environment, published many research papers and supports innovative scientific research. She is a Fellow of the Royal Society of Medicine and more recently as Doctor of Science has been involved in research at Bournemouth University. She is co-author with David Cowan of Ancient Energies of the Earth.

Elizabeth A. Prais is a professional copywriter who works with clients all over the world. In addition to writing, she also acts as a developmental or substantive editor. While her work regularly appears in magazines, websites, and blogs, this is the first published work under her own name.

Charlene K. Haar enjoyed eleven years as a teacher and advisor to Madison, South Dakota high school students in the gifted and talented programme. In 2006, Dr Haar moved to Denham Village from Washington, DC where she was the Founder and President of a research and policy organisation. She is the author and co-author of several books and articles devoted to encouraging competition in education and teacher training through Teach-Now.edu.